With Lyre

and

Bow

A Devotional in Honor of Apollo

Edited by Jennifer Lawrence

BIBLIOTHECA ALEXANDRINA

Apollo by K.S. Roy

3

Dedication

For the Farshooter and Foreseer
Lord of the Wolf and the Raven
and the Mouse and the Locust
Bringer of Health and Plague

Table of Contents

Introduction

by Rebecca Buchanan

Apollo is a God who won my loyalty at a very young age. As a child, I was particularly drawn to Deities of literature, writing, and the wilderness. It was those Goddesses — Athena, Artemis, The Muses — who called to me; and thus Apollo came to my attention, through His connection to The Huntress and the Daughters of Memory. I ignored His darker, more primal aspects, finding it safer to focus on Him as God of poetry and art, the Noble Archer, the Golden Son of Olympus.

As I grew up, and I delved more deeply into Greek mythology, I ran up against those harsher elements more and more frequently. I could not reconcile the Beautiful God I loved with the Flayer of Marsyas, the would-be rapist of Daphne, the Murderer of Niobe's Children.

And so I withdrew. I pushed Apollo away. I stuck with the Goddesses I loved, though, more forgiving of their darker aspects than I was of his; Apollo's ruthlessness, his vindictiveness and lethality, made Him too much of a kind with the Christian God I was struggling to put behind me.

As the years passed, though, and my faith continued to deepen and evolve, I took a second look at Apollo. I reconsidered His history, His relationships with other Deities, His myths and His cults. In so doing, I discovered a God who is marvelously complex, wonderfully complicated, and paradoxically wise, kind, stubborn, and cruel. He is simultaneously virile and earthy, cerebral and transcendent. He is a figure of enlightenment, but also a God of deep passion. He is a God who inspires painful introspection, while also painfully inspiring soul-baring poetry and art.

I have an appreciation now for Apollo's complexity that I did not as a child. I have rediscovered my love for the Son of Leto.

This is a love shared by many of the contributors to this anthology. It is our hope that you find here an expression of the passion you already feel for the God — or that will inspire to explore a relationship with him that you had not previously considered.

Rebecca Buchanan
EiC Bibliotheca Alexandrina
Summer 2016

Songs and Poems

Ἀπόλλων

Apollon by Nicole Lungeanu

Adoration

by Sabina Lungeanu

In the deepest of nights
Are you closest to me, my sun.
All the singing branches of my tree,
All my soul's feathered windows,
My rivers and my boats of dreams
Are reaching out to you.
My world is gently trembling
In expectation of your touch
To call it into life.

An Ever-Burning Lamp

by Hillary Lyon

a wick never trimmed
a light bright as a drop
of sunshine dedicated
to perpetual song

to prophecy and prophetesses
reading water in the bottom
of a well in old Athens tiled
with chants of supplication

or a polished brass bowl in Delphi
rippling with a God's own poetry
a little bit of sun kept
in an ever-burning lamp

hanging unattended in a shadowed niche
leads us like an ancient beacon
down the halls neglected and chaotic
in the crumbling temple of this world

Another Day at the Office for Apollo

by Jon Wesick

Just once I'd like to sleep in. I swear, when I retire, I'm moving to Norway. Buy a little place north of the Arctic Circle and spend six months in glorious darkness. Not that that's going to happen any time soon, especially after Zeus replaced our pensions with 401(k)s. Have you been watching the market? Olive futures tanked and the drachma's in the toilet.

I can never get a decent cup of coffee up here. Zoning board wouldn't let them put in a Dunkin Donuts. Said its décor would clash with the unique character of Mt. Olympus. Really gripes my ass.

Don't get me started on insurance companies. After my son banged up the chariot on his little joy ride, they wouldn't let me take it to the dealer. No! Sent it to some chop shop run by Scythians. Scythians! Now it's supposed to be my fault Helios can't stay in its orbit. Don't blame global warming on me!

And health insurance! Damn pissants told me sunburn is a preexisting condition. It's not like I'm going to die. I'm immortal for Zeus's sake!

What drives me nuts is taxes. I worked hard for everything I got and the government is giving my money away to a bunch of freeloading Dionysians.

The middle class built this mythology and all they're doing is giving us the shaft. Take it from me. The whole cosmology is going down the tubes.

*[Previously published in **Gutter Eloquence**, Issue 29, January 2014. Included here with kind permission.]*

Apollo (13)

by Gareth Writer-Davies

Lucky
Doesn't come into the reckoning

One chance in a million
That the dark eye of the moon

Hid a pantheon of Gods, surly
Long tired of books (the admired past)

It would have been easy
To hurl the mortal pod into the sun

But like argonauts
The shallow, fleeced craft made it home

When all Earth could do
Was make a prayer, an offering of dis-belief

That, so named
The best that we could rend the universe

Would be returned
Burning, an epic voyage of staring, bearded men

Apollon Agetor

by Jessica Orlando

Imposing order,
Capable and commanding,
Arrows at hand,
yet a clear voice of reason calms with sweetly
        chosen words.

You are varied and multi-faceted,
Multi-talented.
You could crush those who disobey your will
        or His will,
A skilled negotiator,
You speak with grace that should not be
        ignored.

Apollo Among the Hyperboreans

by T.J. O'Hare

Beyond the North Wind, my swan-steed bore me
for the winter, along with my Muses,
that they might well restore their melodies
and count the shining hours where naught confuses

in the beauty of these Isles of Radiance.
Rough-hewn, my Temple stands without a roof
and holds as many doors as there may dance
between the columns that demarcate the proof

of Heaven as the Father of us all.
Here, the Sirens learn new songs to coax many
a mariner to forsake his vessel
and find visions where there are not any.

And I am well-accorded with all else
for those who worship me are named the Celts.

Apollo, Lord of Truth

by Jessica Orlando

Apollo, Lord of Truth

Jessica Orlando

♩=110

SA

TB

1. Gol-den son of Le-to, if I could but pour the nec-tar in-to your cup, hang your bow up - on its hook, or sing the prais - es of your name! 2. E - ven the swan sings of you in a clear tone to the beat of her wings as she a - lights

on the bank a-long the ed - dy-ing riv - er. 3. And

you, the sweet - voiced sing - er, with your clear - toned

lyre and nev - er err - ing ar - rows, 4. In ev - 'ry di-

- rec - tion, song has been laid out for you. Fare - well to

you, Lord of Truth. I seek your fav - or with my song.

Apollo of Perdition

by Ellen Denton

Beautiful as the arts you inspire,
whether holding snake or lyre,
marble muscles, curled hair loose,
Apollo, you have been my muse,
walking me through sky and sea
dressed in rose-gilt poesy,
but lately you have come no more
lifting me like an eagle to soar
but rather tortured, feeling damned,
slipping from bed at 2:00 AM,
naked and shivering with the cold
I race to paper and pen to hold
words I saw half in a dream
not to lose them, have them seem
faded in gray light of dawn,
as though for art's sake I'm a pawn.
Your lyre's strings, a prison cage,
holding me in aesthetic rage,
leaving me feeling your serpent's a rod,
and that you're a demon, not a god.

Apollo on the Sibyl

by John J. Brugaletta

She little knew that I had often tongued
through her the prophecies she left on leaves.
From far I saw her sit her tripod's seat,
her vulva open to the earth's sour breath.
It put her in a mind that spread herself
to me, and I took "me" to mean manhood.

I posted Hermes to convey my yes,
but she would trade her offered openness
for two hands filled with sand, and every grain
a year of life for her. She was so young
to have such worries for longevity,
but not so wise that she considered age
in terms of gnawing disabilities,
of flagging flesh and pain at every move.

The bargain closed, and my part her long life,
she still withheld herself and bade me go.
I moved my eye to other virgin flesh,
while she would gloat that she had checked a god.
I cut her off from my predictive mind.

She tried to sell her gnomic leaves for wealth
but burned three-fourths of them before they sold,
which brought my smile. Then at eight hundred
years of age, she begged me for her youth.
I turned my face away. She then began

to pray me that I grant her death, but she
had handed me dry sand instead of her,
and she must now live out her faithless pact
and live to shrink two hundred further years.

Remorse? I don't know what the word denotes.

Archer's Prayer

by Hélio Pires

Hear me, Apollo,
son of Zeus!
Look now,
child of Leto!
My arms,
bent and stretched,
have been raised
from earthly soil to solar field.
I pluck the string of archer's lyre
and in your sight, I pray,
in your honour, I say,
release its note,
the arrow's sting,
with skillful aim
and pious purpose.

Ars Gratia Artis

by Sabina Lungeanu

The song of birds —
such beauty
made for its own sake.
Giver of wings
to those already feather-clad.

Breaking Gold

by Shauna Aura Knight

The words upon my lips
Spiraled out on a breath
The dusky motes of glinted gold
Fell down like sun-dust

Brushed shivers on my skin
The perfect song
To bring that moment
Aching sweet

Flawless gold
That sound of light on
My gilded tongue
Bringing that resonance

That ringing
Resounding echo
Vibrating through my
Amber throat

The prophecy
Falls forth like honey
Words of oracle gold
I must speak the truth

The heartbreak of the words
That frame the future

Poetry or madness
Spinning from my breath

The truth is a song
Of perfect math
The lightning strike to the
Center of the heart

Conflagration

by Mari

summer brilliance
topaz facets incandesce
the setting sun, the temple flame
o god of clarity,
speak truth into my ears
burn me up
in the thunder of your words,
cosmic beauty
which is terror,
fear and trembling

Cyparissus

by Michael Routery

The wind bending these
solemn cypress trees bears
memory of gentle Cyparissus,
he who loved a deer so much
he wished to die himself
when his soft-pelted friend was shot
by careless hunter,
yet, loved as he was by Apollo,
metamorphosed he was into that most
durable of trees, the cypress,
friend of cemeteries;
outlasting death.

Daphne

by Neile Graham

Running from his hunger, my toes snag,
gnarl into the loam and root me. I sway
then steady as they stretch and burrow,
burrow and branch, and branch and branch
again, thrusting between clumps of welcome soil.
Only then the numb heaviness of my sides and
        limbs,
only then the bark shrouding belly and breasts,
the leaves of my hair, discover me. And I reach up,
bark-solid then feathering, reach and stretch
and branch again, to gobble the light and the air.

Hymn to Apollo

by Callum Hurley

My Lord Apollo, bringer of light to all
dark and wanting corners of the musing soul;
be parised, oh lover, brother, Python slayer
rare an' Great Glory of Civilization;
Oh, Golden bringer of heavenly music
in verse, in note and all artly forms to thrall;
to Earth thine rapture, twixst heart and mountaintop
thy gracest mien, ardent be my heart to thine;
Alexicaecus, oh ancient spirit thus
Epicurian upon a pedastool;
By lyre and Bow, your culture in marble froze
With thine sister fair, of Delos born to bare;
An' Pheobus bright for all to see – revere thee
Dulcid, noble, humane, fierce – aspect of thee;
It is of thee mine peer of which song is made
And it is your glory I sing, shining one;
as inspiration densed from Olympus high
beheld in art, fare well good Lord remembered;
of the wise mind shall you always be a par.

Hymn to Apollo

by Jennifer Lawrence

Hail Apollo, Son of Zeus, Son of Leto!
Today let me sing of Your glories,
You whose brightness fills the world,
you who slew the monstrous Python and
made his cave of hidden knowledge
Your holy place of wisdom and foresight.
You whose golden arrows soar from far-off Delos,
striking down the impious, the blasphemous,
the wicked and the greedy, the inhospitable,
and those consumed with arrogance.
Leader of those gifted and beauteous Muses,
You who all arts praise and celebrate,
we greet You with gladness and reverence,
with awe stealing the breath from our throats,
and with gratitude for all You have given us.
You, whose merest touch heals our injuries,
You whose kindness binds our wounds,
and chases the pestilent sicknesses from our frames,
stems the flow of blood when we are hurt,
and in whose name temples of healing were raised.
Let us bring wine and barley to celebrate Your
            name,
let us garland the doorways and burn frankincense,
crown Your statues with laurel boughs,
let us sing to You so long as there
is breath in our lungs, blood in our veins,

and let every gladsome and joyous thought we
       know
come back around to You at last.
O Apollo: Phoebus, Musagetes, Aegletes,
Lyceus, Helius, Cynthius, Acesius, Iatrus,
Apotropaeus and Genetor, Manticus, Hecaërgus:

For each name, a story, a song, and praise,
And all of them I offer to You.

Hymn to Apollo V

by Rebecca Buchanan

they shake their heads in
disbelief
refuse to see the

truth: he came to me
in dawn's light
burning my sickness

away

Hymn to Apollo VII

by Rebecca Buchanan

hunted, i
was born on a
barren island in
a dark sea, the wind
cold: i have not
forgotten

Hymn to Pythios

by Samantha Lykeia Sanders

Musegetes, turn favorable regard upon me as I
      sing of the gods this day,
For I sing of you, great Apollon, who bears the
      instruments of purification.
And there beneath your golden foot disease and
      plague do lay,
There the mighty serpent lies bloodied, dead and
      slain.
Vanquisher of the foul, I sing to you who drives
      plague from the door,
A sacrifice that renews, the blood of the dead
      becomes the living, speaking river.
Hail Apollon, mighty is the sword, the bow and the
      flying arrow,
And those shafts of light that devoured the torn
      flesh of Python,
May they consume and bring to waste the ills
      harbored within men alike.
That which you touch you do strip bare,
That which you see is completely revealed in your
      illumination,
Maddened pestilence, bringer of foul offerings, lays
      exposed.
Your hand does wield the arrow and sword which
      drives it forth,
And your light penetrates all, to rot and decay the
      bloated venomous serpent.

And there the voices rise to sing from the throats of
        women and men, ie paean!
To Pythios, destroyer of the predator pestilence that
        feasts with many mouths upon us.
Rejoice in the death of the plague upon men and his
        beasts, the sickness and gossipy tongue,
The devourer has been shorn of his teeth and claws
        and lies now as dust beneath you.

(Thargelia 2007)

I Am Apollo

by A.J. Huffman

Twin to chastity, I am not
virginity's reflection. I am player
of music, of light. I cannot speak
a lie. Touch me and see

the future.

I Saw a Crow

by A.J. Huffman

fly past midnight.
It waved at the moon as it passed.
I imagined I saw its reflection in the silver
face of this celestial twin, but I blinked
and wings opened to show me the sun.
I breathed as if I had new lungs,
a heavenly gift of perpetuation. I smiled
as the shadow bird dove into waves
of light. I followed
longer than I should have, watched it
shatter into a million falling leaves.
I held
my new-found breath as I fell
into and out of an eternal vision

of my future.

Light of My Heart

by Jessica Orlando

On the seventh day, you stood
My sweet lord of the golden sword
Bright and shining, fierce
in both anger and in love.
You slew Python —
Reasons that were yours alone to judge,
Your aegis-bearing father disagreed.
Yet, you managed His forgiveness.
You took the temple for your own.
Would that I had been born thousands of years
        earlier,
Might I have served you there?
Cloaked my eyes from all the world save for you,
a gorgeous god whom I could never actually see
        with human sight?
Spoken the words that you placed in my mouth with
        your gentle and ethereal tongue?
Your kiss: gentle and strong, unyielding and
        insistent, penetrating
Your inhuman hands – I can feel your touch, but I
        cannot gaze at the way your thumbs
brush my skin. I know the golden curl over your
        forehead quivers when you laugh, yet I
cannot reach up to catch it. Here, only at the edges
        of my senses, then gone, and again
        somewhere else.

You fill my heart, my golden god, yet my heart is
        not all you fill.
My head, my hands, my hips, my throat — each
        part of me exists to please you.
You may do with me as you like.
I'll dance when you wish to see dancers.
I'll lift my voice for your song.
I've learned to pluck your lyre,
yet sometimes I still need your hand to guide my
        own.
I'll unbind my hair and remove my layers when you
        have wishes that gentle girls do not repeat.
Only for you, my radiant one.
For you, I reach into the flame to be kissed by fire.
For you, I'll stand blind in a crowd to speak your
        truth.
For you, I wear your ring and appear wed by those
        who do not understand.
If that temple is raised again, I will be there.
Where you want me, I will be there.
I am your wife to command, though in love, I do
        not hear commands,
only gentle suggestions.
Your life is long, so much longer than my own.
You had time to wait for me,
But now I am here.
For you, the light of my heart, I am here.

Lovesong

by Sabina Lungeanu

You came upon me
Like summer rain at dawn
The nascent day made fertile
By your touch of gold.

Beloved, I am here
My soul's strings all in tune
Awaiting but your fingers
That never come too soon.

Lykeios

by Sabina Lungeanu

I had never known snow until I met you.
Vast, unreachable depths of white
Lashed out by savage gusts of wind.
The rock beneath in slumber lays
And howling creeps in its unquiet dreams.
They will be out tonight, the hunters,
Carving their way into the virgin snow
When Luna rides over the pine tops,
A trail of quiet death will show.
Silence will fall over the land, certain
And ancient as the frozen stars.
How far the stirring and the dance,
A springtime that will never come.

Metaphysics

by Sabina Lungeanu

Yours,
The tensing of the muscle
Every nerve in unison.
Unflinching eyes, gazing
Upon Your victim.
Becoming one
With the feathered flight
Worlds rushing by,
Infinite moments
Divided by Your arrow.

Midwinter

by Sabina Lungeanu

Hail to you, Paian, Shining One,
Borne on the wings of swans
You come to us on Northern winds
From far-off Hyperborea
As you approach, the crows awaken
To greet the rising light
Returned to us from the deep womb
Of the eternal night
Yours is the howling of the wolves
Hunting the sun to be reborn
Come shine on us again, Divine One,
Restore all hope forlorn.

Mississippi Apollo

by Kayleigh Ayn Bohémier

When you finish with that quiver and bow,
Far-Shooter, come to my wide arms, ride
Tributaries to my core like a man tracing
His lover's wrist-veins with warm fingers.
Raise dams of civilization on my banks,
Cover these curves with rock. Press your
Domain up as far as you can: we parent
Civilization here together, you and I,
Father and Mother, civilized and wild.
You walk among the mounds of one hazy
History, tantalizing meticulous seekers,
Dangling flint and ancient burned bones —
That culture feasted us, too, back then.
Lay that bow down gently on my banks,
Pass those shining hands over my murky
Waters until mud sinks and diseases die.
Oracles come and talk gene therapy,
Major and minor scales, conservation,
Big-time developments: all worship me.
Variable, fickle — you teach them to call me
Names when my belly swells and deposits
Fertile mud over commercial farmland,
Provide them with courage to toil and fight
Rising stages, leaching earthen barriers.
Rages like these come and go so quickly.
Above all, when you lay down that quiver,
Sit beside me and teach the tortoise to sing.

My Golden God

by Jessica Orlando

There is no longer a gaping pit
where my heart had once been.
This space has been filled
by the golden light of my golden god.

There is no need to cry myself to sleep
when I can hear Your whispers in my ear
and feel the strength of your arms.

I no longer need love;
I have it.

I will never desperately seek that which is not good
          enough —
someone to try to satisfy a longing
that they cannot touch.

You are that which I longed for.
You are that which I craved.
You are my desire, fulfilled and sated.

Perhaps not wholly sated,
for there could never be enough
of You.

Offering

by Sabina Lungeanu

If I give you
All that I have,
All that I am,
All that I do,
Still, it won't be enough
To repay the gifts
So lavishly bestowed upon me.
Blessed Master,
Giving your children more
Than they could ever hope
To give you in return.

On Delos

by Terence Kuch

One said,
Apollo was not born here
on Delos,
but somewhere else:
Paros, perhaps, or Naxos.

We must make sure
One says this no more:

Loud gold-giving pilgrims hear,

bright Apollo's shrine

dim

"On Delos was bright Apollo born"

by Terence Kuch

The sea off Delos flashed like
trampled glass
each breaker caught
in brilliant air

and then
a liturgy of slivered light —

Now the god is born

Paean

by Sabina Lungeanu

How may I praise you in a song, Beloved,
When poetry itself is what you breathe?
I lay my words bare at your feet,
Virginal blossoms waiting to be picked
And crushed between your fingers into wings.

Nor can I paint the beauty of your face
For colours weren't meant to hold the kind
Of grace that you alone possess,
But let me rather glimpse you in the morn
And the unbearably soft light of dawn.

Phoebus-Apollo Sutra

by T.J. O'Hare

After the sutras had been said
and the mantras recited
with all heartfelt spirituality
Apollo himself came among us
lower-case and radiant
as the most beautiful of youths.
He wore feminine bangles on one wrist
and a masculine strap on the other;
his hair was curly, and his eyes were keen.

He took up his lyre to play;
and the tortoise spirit in the tortoise-shell
added its own eternal gravitas;
and the strings lowed like the white cattle.
And the lyre, because it had first been invented
by a thief, stole away all our hearts
and senses, until only reverence remained.

Oh, Apollo, with your song
grace us with the blessings of your Muses.
Lift up your voice and tax your skillful hands
to wring from those white strings the gifts that
            lift
our hearts and make our feet to dance.

All the lovers that fled from you have longed
for you ever since, and there is not a moment

when their heart obliges with its counter-beat
to the cadence of your over-flowing power.

And when he went
those of us who still stirred
knew that a god had passed among us.
He had walked
among us
with his gospel of dance,
his good news
of music
his *miraaj* of ecstasy
that goes from heart
to heart.

And when the day-song soared with warmth
and delicious light, there he was again
and again
every day
Phoebus-Apollo
in the heavens' sway.

A Poet's Prayer

by Mari

Hail Apollon Aigletos, who shines like the sun,
Musegetes, by any name he wishes to be known.
O god who sheds the light of consciousness,
who opens eyes and minds of prophets and artists,
the touch of your hand sears.
Mark me flame-patterned and scorched,
unfurled to your radiance like a sunflower, exposed.
You are the font of knowledge the Muses shape,
the torch that lights all our lamps.
May inspiration always have your crystalline
        certainty at its root.

Portrait

by Sabina Lungeanu

He is light, and the darkness before light was born
He is life, and the silence preceding it
He is sound, and the stillness before thunderstorms
He is lightning, and the unbearable weight of the air
       before it falls
He is wind, and the infinity of promises held by the
       first bird to stretch its wings
He is movement, and the dreams of dancing that
       young leaves hold in spring
He is time, and the solitude of moments yet unborn.

<u>Prayer</u>

by Sabina Lungeanu

Hail to you, Apollon!
Healer of wounds
I never knew I had.
Light-bringer,
You showed me
What it meant to shine.
Averter of all evil,
My shield through
Dark, cold winter nights.
Maker of music
And of arts
Your song brings harmony to life.
And so I praise you
With my words
And ever in my heart.

Reason

by Terence Kuch

Why am I praying up
to bright Apollo,
sun-blind in the light?

Because the lusty gods
I prayed to
didn't turn that young man's
love to me;
and so at last I'm trying
Reason!

Smintheus

by Steven Klepetar

God of the silver bow,
furious god of plagues,
mouse god, rat god, god
of dust and pyres
and swollen tongues.
How terrible, your flowing hair.
We who danced in joy
at your lyre's tune
and reveled in your
glorious youth, have lived
to see you storming
at heart, your golden brow
dark as rain, your healing
hands red with dire disease.
Our prophet howls
with wolf voice, offerings
burn in reeking smoke of mercy
curdling to a miasma of revenge.

The Song Eternal

by Jason Ross Inczauskis

The Song Eternal sings your praise,
Apollon, Lord of Sound and Light.
It lifts our hearts up all our days,
And leads us through our darkest night.
With your clever rhymes, sacred and sublime,
       please free this mortal race!
That in your glory, we might bask, and gaze upon
       your face!

For all the world's your symphony,
A never ending song!
Your sunlight writes the melody,
The whole world sings along!

The Song Eternal must be heard,
Apollon, Patron of the Arts.
In call of beast and song of bird,
Your music seeps into our hearts.
With your golden lyre, light our passions' fire, and
       free this mortal race!
That in your glory, we might bask, and gaze upon
       your face!

For all the world's your symphony,
A never ending song!
Your sunlight writes the melody,
The whole world sings along!

The Song Eternal flows through all,
Apollon, King of Muses fair,
It echoes through this earthly ball,
In roaring waves and rushing air.
With endless refrains, break these mortal chains,
       and free this mortal race!
That in your glory, we might bask, and gaze upon
       your face!

For all the world's your symphony,
A never ending song!
Your sunlight writes the melody,
The whole world sings along!

A Sonnet for Apollo

by Michael Routery

To offer paeans for Apollo — who
Borne aloft by swan flight, feather-quick,
To winter respite in Hyperborea drew,
The Delphic victor and hero who struck

Against most swollen Python the crusher,
Who sweet whispers in the ears of laurel
Chewing sybils; cities' guide and succor;
He who with wolfish grace averts evil,

Implacable and far shooting brother
Of Artemis; art inspiring Phoebus,
Hyacinthus' lyre-playing lover,
Choir-master of the Parnassian Muses

— Is fit for he has lain beauty for us mortals
Since he first graced pure Delos, immortal.

Sonnet to Apollo

by Audrey Greathouse

With his chariot the sun does arise,
He draws the day up with his fiery horse
And he is the one that prompts the cock's cries,
Dragging the sun by sheer masculine force.
God of the sun and the twin of the night,
His fiery charge we will not dismiss.
Defeating the darkness in noble fight,
Leaving the sunset as a goodnight kiss.
Demeter and Apollo work as one,
He gives plants light as she grows them strong.
To nurture nature with love and sun,
And string his star across the sky with song.
The sun will shine when he starts it to glow,
And so is the mighty god Apollo.

Sun-God's Crown

by Jennifer Lawrence

Whose sweet leaves,
This green hair —
Where has she gone?
I saw her on that riverbank,
Lusted
Pursued
— there never was a sweeter chase —
I heard her call out her father's name.
"Save me!"
That devil, that river-god, that tyrant,
Peneius who loves not love —
Whose magics these are which have
Torn my Daphne away?
No woman born should dare so much,
This disappearance —
Cassandra I punished,
Calliope I loved,
Coronis bore my son.
But this jewel, this prize —
How did I lose her?
I might well wear willow-weeds
(Disconsolate),
But instead I gather emerald fronds,
Lovers'-token,
Almost-what if-might have been —
And weave them for my brow
Her silk, entwined,

Not golden wreath for a locket's heart,
But verdant chaplet for my diadem:
Such hollow victory crown.

To Apollo

by Callum Hurley

My Lord Apollo, oh ancient spirit graced
Oh lover, Theoi, humane Lord
I pray — bringer of art
that thy shining mien;

      your blush, may fill me
        edific; neath a Phoebic light
thine urbane and beautific eye.
And through your rightly arcane ken
      Great Civilization's glory
bringeth to me the truth of things
'tween a stonely past, a future fluid
from the stars unto the tip of pen.

      Show to me; one note
           one score
                one symphony
      But one sincere life upon your lyre's string
And grant to me but your favour
As I have my heart too granted thee;
That my life in rightly sacrament
to good health may be, an' in old age be spared
For many a day
I humbly pray;
          to sit at your study;

student baseborn of grace
close to thine holy rapture brought
bourne upon of art alone.

To Apollon Musagetes

by Samantha Lykeia Sanders

Descending down, like a warm beam to the waiting
earth,
Tender hearts rejoice, welcome and receive him
with joy.
His bow he lays at his golden feet, the arrows set
aside,
Into his hands the lyre draws up, a melody the
strings sing.
To his company Muses, Graces, and Nymphs do
flock,
To sweetly sing and gracefully dance to his
immortal song.
The Horai spin around, their dance the slow wheel
turning,
Ushering the passing of time, and the heavens turn
on course.
And there do the fair-faced goddesses dance, hand
gracing hand,
Among whom stately Athena of the high-crowned
brow dances.
Artemis sets aside torch and bright arrow and bow
to take her place,
Greatly loved of her brother, loved of Nymphs and
loved of dance's song.
And there is winning Aphrodite, dancing among
those beyond her touch,

Her dance in the winsome song of love, that sways
        listening hearts.
But no influence of the heart is greater than
        Musagetes' own lifting song!
Most holy god of the lyre, most beloved leader of
        the light-voiced Muses,
The heavens, earth, and sea bow before your
        trembling strings.
They sweeten and shake the vaulted skies, and
        soothe the restless earth,
The clawed lion lays down submissively beneath
        that thrumming light.
You who turn hearts and minds by the message of
        your lulling song,
I pray that your song join to me, by your will to sing
        of the immortal gods!
From your hand you send down Terpsichore to
        whisper holy hymn,
Into the waiting ear that receives your golden song,
        and sings it again.
Great inspirer, these hands that write, my mortal
        hands never err,
When composing and weaving the arts of fable,
        story, lore, and holy hymn.
I pray that I communicate in clear voice a song
        worthy of your love,
And that it fall upon the earth and be remembered
        for this short mortal time.

Transported

by Gary Beck

I sing a poem of love
inspired by your cello voice
that leaves my insides tingly
and find myself fluted
by Ionic columns,
to temples of elation.

We Address

by Hillary Lyon

The beauty of the beardless youth
in bronze, in marble, in paint
on the walls of ancient
tombs and temples

encouraging the loyal
rituals of sacrifice and song,
of poetry and perfume.
Oh where are you now

with your lyre and bow,
with your art and oracles,
with your crown of piercing rays.
Either disguised or reinvented,

have you not returned?
Or is it that you never left?
Such breath-taking beauty compels
the modern world to ask:

Are you Phoebus?
Are you Christ? Are you the one
who'll drive our fiery chariots
into the uncharted regions of heaven?

Essays

The Sun and Ocarina by Callum Hurley

Apollo's Demon Dagger

by John Opsopaus, PhD

The Avar Skywalker

In the sixth century BCE, before the beginning of classical Greek civilization, a mysterious man was traveling in a circle encompassing Greece, not stopping to eat or drink except at the sanctuaries of the Gods. He traveled swift as the wind — some said his feet didn't touch the ground — banishing pestilence and purifying the land. He held a peculiar sort of golden arrow, by which he traveled. They said he was possessed by Apollo and came as a prophet and envoy from Hyperborea, the land beyond the North Wind especially dear to Apollo (most likely northern Asia).

His name was Abaris, which simply means "the Avar," referring to the nomadic bowmen of Mongolia. This is according to classical scholar Peter Kingsley's exquisite and well-documented book, *A Story Waiting to Pierce You*, a source for much of this chapter. Abaris was called a Skywalker (Grk. *aithrobatês*), the Greek translation of words common in Tibet and Mongolia to describe shamans, but also arrows (e.g., Tib. *khandro*).

One early account of the Avar Skywalker says that Apollo himself had given him the arrow, which was made of gold and unusually bulky. But the Greek word *belos*, often translated "arrow," can also refer to a dart, javelin, bolt, or any terrifying missile that strikes from afar. (One of Apollo's common epithets is *Hekatêbolos* — Far-Darter — for his arrows strike out of nowhere, bringing pestilence, but also sudden cures, inspiration, and illumination.) *Belos* can also refer to a sword, and Kingsley argues that Abaris' golden "arrow" was a Phurba, the three-bladed ritual dagger of Mongolian and Tibetan shamans, of Tibetan Buddhists, and of Indian Vedic practitioners. As will be explained shortly, it is simultaneously arrow, dart, dagger, and stake.

To traverse the thousands of miles from Hyperborea to Greece, Abaris would have traveled in an ecstatic trance, like the Tibetan "wind walkers," whose feet scarcely touch the ground, if at all. Complete inner stillness and control of subtle energies (using *lung-gom-pa*, the "wind-energy meditation") enables superhuman outer abilities. He would have flown across the landscape, carried by his Phurba, held in front, in the same way that water witches are dragged about by their willow wands.

Apollo had given Abaris the golden arrow as a token of divine sanction. Ancient sources say he was an ambassador from the Hyperboreans, which is unsurprising when we learn that Mongol ambassadors were sent with a golden arrow as a token of trust from the Khan, often to confer spiritual authority on its recipient. These envoys fly like magical arrows to their destinations, penetrating all obstructions, finding their way unerringly. Ancient sources say explicitly that Abaris traveled in a circle around Greece, and the Mongols called their envoys "arrow circulators," which is also how they were described by Chinese observers (*chuanjian, chuanjian dahua, chuanjian tonghua*).

What was Abaris' mission? By definition, a new era, a revolution in thought, cannot grow out of the dichotomies and structures — the being — of the past, which delimit and constrain possibility. The future must be created afresh by those who are able to journey to the undifferentiated ground that underlies being and to bring back a new dispensation from the Gods and the ancestors. This is the task of the Skywalkers, who visit Heaven and the Underworld, and then become the Arrow Circulators, who cast a sacred circle round a land and consecrate it to a new destiny. What destiny did Abaris bring?

Pythagoras, who lived in the sixth century BCE, holds a unique position in the history of Western science and esotericism, for the Pythagoreans understood numbers both scientifically and mystically, a unified view lost to contemporary science. The Pythagorean influence was profound. Both Copernicus (who called his heliocentric model "the Pythagorean theory") and Newton (whose was obsessed with occult forces and alchemy) appealed to ancient Pythagorean ideas. But these are just two examples, for this

2600-year-long river of thought and practice runs deep in the Western tradition.

Ancient biographies tell us that the Delphic Oracle predicted Pythagoras' birth and that in fact he was the son of Hyperborean Apollo. (His name refers to "the Pythian," that is, to Apollo.) These biographies also say that Abaris came to Pythagoras and gave him the golden *belos*, conferring on him the authority to, in effect, establish the European scientific, esoteric, and spiritual traditions. Abaris also confirmed that Pythagoras had a golden thigh, evidence of a shamanic initiation, in which the future shaman's body is torn to pieces and reassembled, but with one human part made divine. Many of Pythagoras' teachers and students displayed shamanic abilities, including being in two places at once, traveling to spirit realms in trance, journeying on a magic dart, accompanying Apollo as a bird, and remembering past lives. Indeed, Pythagoras could identify objects he had owned in previous incarnations. This is, of course, one of the techniques by which a reincarnated spiritual or worldly leader (Tib. *tulku*) is identified; the Dalai Lama is the best-known example.

Pythagoras founded a spiritual fellowship devoted to promoting a better way of life for people as individuals, in community, and in the state. He even coined a word for their Love of Sophia (Wisdom): *philo-sophia.* For in the ancient world philosophy was not a sterile academic study; it was a way of life built around ethical behavior, spiritual practices, and mystical experience. Pythagoreanism is the fountainhead of most of Western mysticism, especially of the theurgical practices for invoking the Gods. (See my "Summary of Pythagorean Theology.") This tradition is central to the destiny of Western civilization, but it has been marginalized for many centuries in favor of strict materialism.

Symbolism

A traditional Phurba is divided into three distinct parts: the pommel, the handle, and the blade: its head, body, and feet (see the figure). Symbolically these correspond to the three realms of shamanic cosmology: the heavens, earth, and the underworld. Appropriately, the shaman grasps the Phurba by its handle (the human realm) and holds it like a dagger, with the blade downward.

From a Pythagorean perspective, the three parts of the Phurba also represent the three realms of (1) spirit or mind (which is eternal and of the essence of the divine), (2) the soul (which brings the divine into active manifestation in time and space), and (3) matter (which is animated by the soul). These three levels structure the macrocosm as a whole and are mirrored in the microcosms of individual people. In this way the shaman identifies with the Phurba.

For Tibetan Buddhists the upper half of the Phurba (pommel and handle) represents nirvana, and the blade represents samsara (the illusory world of the senses). As a whole the Phurba symbolizes their union in a single primordial nature, the Ineffable One, the awareness of which is the essence of wisdom.

Although there are many kinds of Phurbas, the pommel usually has three faces, representing three aspects of Vajrakilaya (Tib. Dorje Phurba) — the deity governing and immanent in the Phurba. (Kilaya is a form of Sanskrit *kila*, which translates Tibetan *phurba*; *vajra kila* means "unshakable or indestructible *phurba*.") The three faces are Vajrakilaya's joyful, peaceful, and wrathful aspects (a compassionate wrath that destroys dualistic delusions, obstructions, and other negative influences by transmuting them into wisdom). This is, however, just one of the many layers of meaning. For example, the faces also represent Buddha's "threefold body" (Skt. *trikaya*): his individual mortal personality, his timeless Buddha nature, and his spiritual joy in teaching. They also represent the basis, path, and result of spiritual practice. Above the three faces is a unifying symbol, such as a half-vajra (half-thunderbolt), symbolizing enlightenment, the indestructible nature of awareness. A Pythagorean might see the three aspects of the Ineffable One: Existence, Life, and

81

Mind, which recur in various guises throughout the divine realms.

The handle of the Phurba takes the form of a stylized thunderbolt (Skt. *vajra*, Tib. *dorje*), although it is often represented as tied with cloth or "eternal knots." This is appropriate for the human realm, for our souls are embodied; the divine spark is bound and hidden inside. It also protects holders who might not be fully qualified and empowered to wield the Phurba.

The blade has three triangular faces, thereby incorporating the divine numbers Three and Nine. For Buddhists the blade represents the "three poisons" that block spiritual progress: (1) desire and excessive attachment, (2) aversion, fear, and anger, and (3) delusion and ignorance (from which the other two arise). In an instant these three demons can be ensnared by the Phurba's blade and banished through its point, which represents the one-pointed concentration of the fully enlightened mind that has penetrated all obstructions and obscurity. Thus the Phurba is thrust firmly into the earth like a tent stake. The staked demons are immobilized but not destroyed, so their power may be transmuted and used constructively. Negative mental states are liberated from duality and dissolved into the undifferentiated ground of primordial nature: supreme awareness wisdom (which is also Vajrakilaya). This wisdom reveals that these mental states have no inherent existence; they are "empty." Vajrakilaya neutralizes obstacles as the sun dispels obscurity and darkness, or as Apollo's bright arrows purify whatever they strike.

The faces of the blade are decorated usually with serpents (the Nagas), especially two intertwined serpents reminiscent of Hermes' caduceus. The blade may flow from the mouth of a monster (often the makara, an elephant-crocodile chimera), whose head surmounts the blade. Thus the blade represents the subterranean waters and the monsters that dwell therein. But the monster's mouth, which is at the Phurba's navel, unites nirvana (represented by the phurba's upper part) with samsara (represented by the blade) and symbolizes the compassion that enlightened beings pour onto unliberated beings. It removes obstacles for those who have wandered off the path of enlightenment.

The symbolism is similar in Pythagorean philosophy, for Hades, the Underworld, is a symbol of the material world — the world of demonic distractions — in which everything is in flux, and thus symbolized by water. In Greek myth, Apollo killed the Python, a subterranean monster, and built his Delphic temple upon its body. He killed the chthonic dragon with his golden arrows, which Aeschylus called "winged serpents" (Grk. *ptênos ophis*). Delphi is considered the World's Navel, from which the Pythia, the Delphic oracle, makes her pronouncements.

Many think the original use of the Phurba was as a tent stake. As such it is an instrument of stability, in the mind as well as in the physical world. It establishes the bounds of the tent, and therefore is also used for establishing sacred space, immobilizing all malignant forces, especially those coming from below.

Like the shamanic World Tree, the Phurba is planted in the Center, the Cosmic Axis, the Navel of the Earth. Its pommel is the crown of the World Tree, its handle the trunk, and its blade the roots, penetrating and grounded in Mother Earth. Therefore, the Phurba is the means by which the shaman journeys on the Cosmic Tree, ascending up the trunk into the Heavens or down its roots into the Underworld.

The Samoyeds of Siberia saw the Pole Star, which marks the cosmic axis, as the "Sky Nail" that anchors the canopy of the sky, like a macrocosmic tent, to Earth. Thus the Phurba is a symbol of the cosmic pillar penetrating the Earth at Her navel. Mountains, which are natural comic pillars joining Heaven and Earth, are called "Phurbas of the Earth" (Tib. *sa-yi phurba*). For practitioners of Bön (pre-Buddhist Tibetan shamanism) the Phurba was also a symbol of the lightning bolt striking the Earth and of the rays of the Sun. Consistent with these images of power descending from Heaven, meteoric iron, which they called "Sky Iron," was prized for making Phurbas (although Phurbas of different materials and colors are used for different purposes). Therefore, the Phurba is the magical dart or arrow shot by a God from Heaven to Earth, bringing the Divine into the human realm.

The Phurba thus represents illumination from Heaven — the Sun's rays — Apollo's arrows. But if the arrow-rays descend from Heaven to Earth, they also provide the ladder by which one may ascend to the Heavens. As shamans from many cultures shoot arrows into the Sun, so the Phurba becomes an instrument by which they ascend to the celestial realms.

The archer twins Apollo and Artemis are distant deities; they act from afar. Their arrows symbolize the rays of the sun and moon, respectively, and their divine powers. Both Gods are known by the epithet *Hekatêbolos* (sometimes shortened to *Hekêbolos*), which the ancients interpreted to mean Far-darter, from *hekas* (far, far off, afar) and *bolos* (a throw or cast). Moreover, Apollo is called Hekatos and Artemis is called Hekatê, masculine and feminine forms referring to their distance from us. This suggests a connection between the Goddesses Artemis and Hekatê, who are closely related lunar deities and relevant to our investigation.

The Chaldean Oracles are an inspired text dictated by the Goddess Hekatê and fundamental to the practice of divine ascent taught by Pythagoras' Neoplatonic successors. She has a special role, because she is identified with the World Soul and brings the immaterial Ideas into material manifestation, thus creating the natural world, through her "Lightning-Storm-receiving Wombs of Radiant Light" (fr. 35), "the Womb Life-Giving of Hekátê" (C.O. fr. 32). Moreover, because she rules the lunar sphere, which is the lowest celestial sphere, she is the Ruler of Daimons (*Daimoniarkhês*), for they occupy the sublunary realm. All the Gods have daimons, who are their assistants and messengers, but Hekatê is especially responsible for the Material Daimons, known as the Dogs of Hekatê, for she is

the Driver of the Dogs of Water, Earth, and Air.
(C.O. fr. 91)

The Material Daimons are not evil, but it is their cosmic role to convey the Ideas into material embodiment, and so they are impediments to the ascent who must be pacified. Therefore, the Phurba is used to immobilize them. In the Oracles (fr. 2) the theurgist is instructed:

when thou hast donned the Vigor full-arrayed of Sounding Light,
and hast equipped thy mind and soul with Three-barbed Strength,
then cast the Triad's whole Sign in thy breast, and haunt
Empyrean channels, not dispersed, but gathered in.

That is, invoke Apollo, Lord of Cosmic Harmony, to fill your mind (Grk. *nous*) and soul with his illumination and triple strength so you can rise up on the rays of the Ineffable One. Riding the Phurba to ascend the rays of the spiritual Sun is equivalent to allowing it to carry you into the depths of your soul, to pierce your inmost heart, which Pythagoreans call the Central Fire, around which your psyche orbits.

Ritual Use

I will mention briefly some ways to use the Phurba in ritual and spiritual practice. However, I'm obliged to mention some cautions. Abusing the powers of the Phurba will be at best ineffective, but can rebound seven-fold against the Phurba's wielder, and even against their family, friends, and the wider community. This is why, in Tibetan Buddhism, practice with the physical Phurba is built on three prerequisite Phurba practices: the awareness-wisdom Phurba, the immeasurable-compassion Phurba, and the *bodhichitta* Phurba (*bodhichitta* being the enlightened heart, uniting love and compassion). Without a solid spiritual and ethical foundation, practicing magic is foolhardy.

As cosmic tent stake, world pillar, and nail to immobilize demons, the Phurba is a tool of stable awareness and one-pointed concentration. Hold the Phurba, point downward, between your palms in "prayer position." Meditate on its stability and ability to fix consciousness, anchoring it at the world axis. Vajrakilaya may bring you awareness of the non-dual ground of everything.

The Phurba may be used more actively to banish obstructions on the path to enlightenment. Holding it like a dagger, but with just the thumb and middle two fingers (like the "horns sign"), use it to ensnare all impediments on the blade, and to transform them into emptiness at the point, which you can plunge into the ground or into a basket or bowl of rice. The Phurba can be used for other kinds of healing, manipulating vital energies and subtle bodies, grounding out malignant forces. The top of the pommel, which represents supreme wisdom and compassion, is used for blessing.

In traditional Tibetan Buddhist practice, negative spirits (especially ignorance) are invited to accept generous offerings of primordial wisdom, in order to transmute them to positive spirits. They are banished if they are too strong to be transmuted at that time. Then, a protective boundary or wheel (Tib. *sung khor*) is cast. The five wind-energies, which correspond to the five elements, are projected as the layers of a protective tent, each contributing its characteristic power of protection. (In the Western tradition, Earth is inmost, followed by Water, Air, Fire, and Æther.)

In a Tibetan Vajrakilaya visualization, the practitioner identifies with Vajrakilaya in order to banish the four demons (concerned with the aggregates, the emotions, death, and the Gods). The Palace of Vajrakilaya arises out of the undifferentiated ground of being, which is represented by the Tibetan or Sanskrit letter for E, since *Eka* is the Sanskrit word for "One." Interestingly, Apollo's temple at Delphi had the Greek letter E on it, which the ancients were at a loss to explain; perhaps it referred to the ineffable One (Grk. *EN*, pronounced "hen"). Next, the visualization follows an upward 4-3-2-1 pattern reminiscent of the Pythagorean sacred symbol, the Tetractys (a triangular arrangement of ten dots, 4-3-2-1 from bottom to top). In the center of the palace is a four-spoke wheel, like a throwing-star. The four spokes are the "great gate keepers," the boundless meditations on love, compassion, joy, and equanimity. Above the wheel is a triangular platform, representing the "three doors of liberation" (basis, path, and result). Above this are symbols of duality: sun and moon disks and male and female demons; the male represents anger and the female attachment (Ares and Aphrodite in Hellenic tradition). Above them is the figure of Vajrakumara (Tib. Dorje Zhönu), whose name means Indestructible Youth. This is an alter ego of Vajrakilaya, and recalls Apollo's ancient and regular representation as a youth. Vajrakumara's right hand holds a Vajra scepter upward (skillful means), and his left a Phurba downward (wisdom). With his wings he can fly everywhere and penetrate any obstacle. Joined with him in sexual union is his consort Diptachakra (Tib. Khorlo Gyedeb), who represents Secret Wisdom (Grk. Sophia or Gnôsis), which complements his Awareness; her knife severs ego-clinging and neurosis. The Phurba is the nail of primordial wisdom, which makes the visualization stable and firm.

The Kilaya Tantra says that the universe and everything in it has the form of the Phurba, which is thus a universal symbol; it has a head, body, and feet, just like a person. When shamans are about to journey, they hold the Phurba and identify with it; they become the Phurba. Then they can journey, like the dart, wherever required, swiftly penetrating all obstacles to reach their goal. Shaman and arrow are both called Skywalker, because they are one.

That is enough for now. As the Tibetans' Guru Rinpoche asked, "Now that you know what the Phurba is, where will you put it?"

*[Author's Note: An earlier version of this chapter appeared in **Circle Magazine**, issue 108, Spring 2011, pp. 10–12. Included here with kind permission.]*

Bibliography

Kingsley, Peter. *A Story Waiting to Pierce You: Mongolia, Tibet, and the Destiny of the Western World.* Point Reyes: Golden Sufi, 2010.

Majercik, Ruth. *The Chaldean Oracles: Text, Translation, and Commentary.* Leiden: E. J. Brill, 1989.

Opsopaus, John. "Select Chaldean Oracles." http:// omphalos.org/BA/SCO.html

Opsopaus, John. "Summary of Pythagorean Theology." http://omphalos.org/BA/ETP

Palden Sherab, Khenchen, and Tsewang Dongyal, Khenpo. *The Dark Red Amulet: Oral Instructions on the Practice of Vajrakilaya.* Ithaca: Snow Lion, 2008.

As Bright as the Sun:
Comparing Apollo and Freyr

by Hélio Pires

Freyr is the most glorious of the Æsir. He is ruler of rain and sunshine and thus of the produce of the earth and it is good to pray to him for prosperity and peace. — Edda: Gylfaginning 24 (Faulkes 2000: 24)

It is with these words that the thirteenth-century Icelander Snorri Sturluson presents the god Freyr. The image they convey is that of a fertility deity, though far from being limited to an earthly realm, He also has influence over the skies. What follows is a very brief overview of the god, his many sides — both ancient and modern — and how that may connect Him with Apollo. This is not an attempt at showing that they are the same deity, since I believe them to be separate entities. But when two gods show several similarities and their domains overlap considerably, there is ground for collaborative syncretism: just as two men are not one and they may nonetheless own a business together and share a work contact, so too different gods may collaborate on common issues under an equally common form, in this case Apollo-Freyr or vice-versa. Or they may simply be worshipped side by side as separate figures. Both ways are possible and I will not side with one or the other. My goal here is merely to highlight the similarities between the two deities, which is also part of my effort to create a Latinized cult of Freyr, something that can benefit from bridges between the Norse and the Mediterranean worlds.

The Golden Lord of Boars

Freyr is an ancient Germanic god. Given the lack of early written sources or obvious iconography, it is unclear how old his cult is, but its origins may stretch back to the centuries before the Common Era.

While it is impossible to be sure, the hints can be found in Tacitus' *Germania*, written by the end of the first century CE. In it, it is said that the Germanic tribes traced their origins to a god called Tuisto, born from the soil, and his son Mannus, who in turn had three sons, who then founded and named different sets of tribes: those closest to the sea were called Ingaevones, the central communities were the Herminones and the remaining ones were the Istaevones (Hutton and Warmington 2000: 130-1). Of interest here is the first of the three, since the name includes the element *ing-*, which in later sources is associated with Freyr. Snorri Stulurson, for instance, calls Him Yngvi-Freyr (Faulkes 2000: 156; Hollander 1999: 14) and it seems the ancient Swedish dynasty of the Ynglings, another name starting with *ing-*, considered Him to be their divine ancestor. It is unclear if Yngvi is an old name for the god, since Freyr is actually a title meaning "lord", or if they were originally two deities who at some point became associated and blended. Tacitus also mentions a Scandinavian people called *Suiones*, which corresponds to the Norse *Svear*, who lived around lake Mälar and formed the core of Sweden. In fact, the name of the country derives from the expression *Svea rike* — the realm of the *Svear* – and in *Germania* it is told that the *Suiones* worshiped the mother of the Gods, whose emblem was the wild boar (Hutton and Warmington 2000: 206-7). Which is interesting, because in the surviving Norse myths that same animal is associated with Freyr and there's a concentration of Freyr-related placenames in Sweden, namely around the lake Mälar, suggesting that at some point He was a popular deity in the region (Brink 2007: 109-11). Of course, Tacitus mentions a goddess, not a god, and there is a huge chronological gap between the *Germania* on one end and late medieval sources on the other, so it's hard to get a clear picture of Freyr's origins, the context of his cult, and its evolution. The only certainty is the existence of a linguistic and symbolic continuum that can be traced back to the first century CE and may presumably be older than that.

What the Old Norse sources tell us about Freyr is that He is one of the Vanir, a tribe of gods that is commonly seen as presiding over peace, Nature, and fertility, which, in my opinion, is a simplistic view. That, however, is another matter

94

altogether, so suffice to say that the Vanir are best described as gods of sovereignty and general prosperity, two ideas that cannot be separated, since one's independence requires means to sustain it.

Freyr has a twin sister called Freya – another title, this meaning "lady" — a goddess of lust, riches, magic, war, and death, all areas that fall well within the symbolic universe of the boar.

And their father is Njord, a deity of ships and everything associated with them, from the wind and sailable waters to the wealth they provide.

Freyr's mother, however, is a tricky subject, as nowhere in the surviving Norse texts is She clearly mentioned and there are conflicting traditions on Her identity, with some sources indicating the mountain giantess Skadi and others talking of an unnamed sister of Njord. Incest, it appears, is seen as normal among the Vanir. It is not impossible that Freyr's mother is the Germanic goddess whom Tacitus calls Nerthus (Hutton and Warmington 2000: 196-7), which is a linguistic equivalent of the Old Norse *Njörðr* (Simek 2000: 230), or the mother of the gods of the *Suiones*, in which case Freyr would have inherited her sacred animal. The two goddesses may even be one and the same, but the chronological gap between *Germania* and the other sources cuts the strength of any theory that seeks to connect Tacitus' writings with much later texts.

Freyr is also associated with the Elves, since stanza five of the eddic poem *Grímnismál* says He

95

was given Alfheim, the Elf-land or home, as a teething gift. Who those Elves are exactly, if nature spirits, deceased humans, demi-gods or a mixture of all three is unclear, since the word *alfar* is used rather liberally in Norse sources and folklore, and nothing else is told about that episode of Freyr's infancy.

In another instance in the surviving mythology, He was also given a magic vessel called Skidbladnir, which, appropriately for a son of Njord, is referred to as *skipa betzt* or "the best of ships" in stanza forty-three of *Grímnismál*. And Freyr received a golden boar as well, normally called Gullinbursti or "Golden Bristles", though it has been suggested that that is merely a description which was misinterpreted as a name for the god's animal (Lindow 2001: 277-8). Freyr had another treasure, a sword that fought on its own, but He is said to have given it away out of love for a giantess, in what has been interpreted by some as a symbolic castration.

On that note, He seems to have a strong following among the pagan and polytheist LGBT community, which goes well with what appears to be the Vanir's open stance on sexuality and Freyr's phallic nature. This latter aspect of His is indicated by Adam of Bremen's description of the pagan temple of Uppsala, which, so says the text, housed images of the gods, including one Frikko, who was depicted in an ithyphallic fashion (Tschan 2002: 207). It is presumed that Frikko is a Latinized form of Freyr, but in any case a visible and preferably large phallus is only to be expected in a deity that's strongly associated with fertility, as indicated by the quote from Snorri's *Edda* at the start of this text.

Also mentioned in the same quote is Freyr's connection to peace. The original Old Norse word is *friðr*, which is often translated precisely as "peace," but this runs the risk of being simplistic, for *friðr* implies the notion of protection and assistance. It is "the state or condition prevailing among those who regard each other as their own kindred" (Green 1998: 43), which is another way of saying that it stands for family and social stability, the very condition that allows communities to prosper. To paraphrase a Harrison Ford movie character, peace is not merely the absence of conflict, but the presence of justice, and that is what *friðr* is: the presence of the network of rights and duties that sustains peace.

Make no mistake: Freyr is not a non-violent god! It's true that He's generally peaceful and joyous and there are modern accounts of how He has filled people with a nurturing warmth. Freyr radiates life-force and indeed He's called *bjartur* or "bright" in stanza fifty-three of the eddic poem *Völuspá*, *skírom* or "shining" in stanza forty-three of *Grímnismál*. But He is not above the use of overwhelming force if it comes to it. Think of Him along the lines of a parliament's sergeant-in-arms, in that He ensures the peace in a place where physical violence is forbidden — and in the ancient world, assembly sites were often hallowed ground, which in Old Norse would be called *friðrgarðr* or "sacred enclosure" — but He will use force if that's what it takes to keep things in order. There are actually several hints at Freyr's military side in the old sources, though most people tend to overlook it: in the skaldic poem *Hrafnsmál*, the kenning *Freys leik* or Freyr's game has been interpreted as meaning "battle", which has intrigued scholars (Abram 2011: 94); in Snorri's *Edda*, He's called *böðfróðr*, which means "battle-skilled" or "battle-wise" (Faulkes 2000: 75); according to the same source, his golden boar is also called Slíðrugtanni or "dangerous tooth" (Faulkes 2000: 50) and it is told that Freyr killed a giant named Beli, something which, so says Snorri, the god could have done using nothing more than his fists (Faukes 2000: 32).

It is perhaps His animal that best sums up Freyr's nature, for the boar is simultaneously a symbol of fertility, abundance, and fighting qualities, being a creature that reproduces easily, was a traditional source of meat, and which will slash and trample in a deadly fashion, though it often prefers to avoid combat. It is only when provoked or threatened that a boar is likely to strike with deadly intent and that is how it is with Freyr: if needed, He will fight and do so skillfully; otherwise, expect Him to be generous and peaceful. It is not by chance that He is also called *veraldargoðr* or "god of the world" (Hollander

1999: 14), i.e. of all things necessary for worldly happiness and well-being.

North Meets South

Having briefly presented Freyr, some of his links with Apollo are probably already evident, but others require some work, combined with a considerable degree of modern gnosis and a reinterpretation of the god in a Mediterranean context.

The first obvious element is that both have a twin sister, though Artemis and Freya differ greatly in matters of intimate behaviour; for while the former is a virginal goddess, the latter is lustful. In sexual terms, She's a Norse Aphrodite and Loki makes that clear in stanzas thirty and thirty-two of the eddic poem *Lokasenna*, where He accuses Freya of having had sex with every god and elf, including her own brother.

Also obvious is the radiant nature of the two gods, since both Freyr and Apollo are associated with the sun and presented as bright or shining.

And on a similar note, they stand for an ideal of physical beauty, with Snorri's *Edda* stating that the twin children of Njord are beautiful in appearance (Faulkes 2000: 24).

Finally, another obvious point is that both gods share a link with the sea, though the aquatic element is not their primary realm: Freyr owns the best of ships and his father is a god of vessels, winds and waterways; Apollo is connected to harbours, mariners, and dolphins.

A more complex issue is their rural aspect, which has multiple ramifications. Farming and the agricultural cycle are at the heart of Freyr's identity, which is unsurprising in a god who makes things grow, be it crops, human and animal numbers, prosperity, life in general, or certain parts of the male anatomy. Apollo, however, is not Demeter, so his role in the sprouting of seeds and increase of crops is limited. But He is not without a connection with shepherds and flocks, so at that rural level the two gods meet.

At the same time, because Freyr relates to the agricultural cycle, it is safe to assume that He understands the need for renewal, of how life feeds on life and the old must make way for the new. This is a basic dynamic in the natural world, where summer is followed by winter and then summer again, crops grow and wither before growing once more, death and decay provide room and fertilizer for fresh life.

A god of the bounty of the earth is likely to be aware of this and it resonates with Apollo's role as a destroyer and renovator, the raven god who cleanses. It doesn't mean that they're both deities of purification and health, since Freyr lacks any known connection with the medical arts, which in Norse mythology are the realm of the goddess Eir.

Though it could be argued that because He is god of the world, provider of things needed for worldly well-being, Freyr and Apollo can collaborate on matters of health, which cannot be sustained without proper nourishment. But most importantly, in their own way, they're both gods of renewal and I'd go as far as saying that, on that note, the boar is to Freyr what the raven is to Apollo: both swines and corvids are omnivorous, known to consume dead flesh, and for centuries pigs were commonly used as living trash bins. They were kept close by and fed organic trash, which was thus easily disposed of, so just as the raven eats away the old, so does the great boar. In their own way, swines cleanse and, contrary to the popular misconception, they're not the dirtiest of animals.

When placing Freyr in a Latin context, you also get another side of Him that can be connected with Apollo: averter of evil or *Alexikakos*. And the reason is a phallic one. Literally! A phallus was a common apotropaic symbol in Mediterranean cultures, as shown by multiple archaeological pieces. One of my favourites is a wind chime that's on display in the British Museum and which depicts a penis with wings, the back body of a lion and a supplementary penis between the legs (because you can never get enough genitalia). And since Freyr is a phallic god, as is to be expected from a male fertility deity, it seems only natural that once you place Him in a Mediterranean context, He will also assume a role of averter of evil, protecting both people and goods. This is reinforced by his connection with *friðr* which, when applied to sacred or enclosed spaces, has the sense of holiness or sacred inviolability. Again, consider the metaphor of the sergeant-at-arms, in effect the guardian of a parliament and the keeper of its inviolable status, if necessary by force. We had a recent example of just that with the 2014 attack on the Canadian parliament, were the shooter was killed by the assembly's sergeant. And this also allows for a connection between Freyr and Apollo as guardians of boundaries, namely sacred ones.

There is also the issue of homosexuality and homoeroticism, with which the brother of Artemis is commonly associated, though how far that resulted in an apollonian blessing of male-male love in the ancient world is unclear to me. In any case, even if the link was not as common as imagined today, it nonetheless exists in the modern world and the same can be said about Freyr who, as mentioned, appears to attract a considerable amount of gay men. And that, I'd argue, derives both from his nature as one of the Vanir and his connection with *friðr* as the protective ties of kinship: it doesn't matter if you love someone of the same or opposite sex, so long as both parties do so freely and create bonds of mutual assistance and devotion. And just as today Apollo may bless same-sex marriages, so can Freyr.

There are of course areas where they do not overlap. Prophecy is one of them, though Freya, being a goddess of magic and especially of the form of Norse magic known as *Seiðr*, is a seer in her own right. Considering how the two of them have so much in common, being twins and all, one wonders how much of the Vanir arts are known to Freyr. But, at least to my knowledge, He has no prophetic role. He also has no connection with music, poetry or any similar art, which in the Norse world would be the realm of the gods Odin and Bragi. It's true that Freyr is called *fróði*, which means "wise" or "well-learned," but that may relate more to his role as keeper of the peace, which requires the presence of justice and hence of wise judgments. And apart from the Elves, assuming that an elf of Alfheim is of the bow-and-arrow type, He also has no link to archery.

As with any comparison, you never get a complete match between the two sides. There will always be differences, even if minor ones, derived from either cultural context or the fact that, despite being very close, they're different gods. The latter is, I believe, the case with Freyr and Apollo.

And yet they overlap on so many things that, once you put Freyr in a Mediterranean context, collaborative syncretism between him and Apollo seems almost like a natural option. One that is symbolically reinforced by the mythology of the latter: after all, isn't the land of the Hyperboreans in the north? And isn't Freyr a god native to the northernmost part of Europe?

Bibliography

Primary sources

Faulkes, Anthony, ed. 2000. *Snorri Sturluson. Edda.* Everyman's Library, 6th edition, London: Dent.

Hollander, Lee M. ed. 1999. *Snorri Sturluson. Heimskringla: History of the kings of Norway,* 3rd edition, Austin: Texas University Press.

Hutton, M. and Warmington, E. H. eds. 2000. "Germania" in *Tacitus. Agricola, Germania, Dialogus,* Loeb Classical Library 35, 13th edition, Cambridge, Massachusetts, London: Harvard University Press, 117-215.

Tschan, Francis, ed. 2002. *Adam of Bremen. History of the Archbishops of Hamburg-Bremen,* New York: Columbia University Press.

Secondary sources

Abram, Christopher. 2011. *Myths of the pagan north: the gods of the Norsemen,* London, New York: Continuum.

Brink, Stefan. 2007. "How uniform was the old Norse religion" in *Learning and understanding in the old Norse world. Essays in honour of Margaret Clunies Ross,* eds. Judith Quinn et al. Turnhout: Brepols, 105-136.

Green, D.H. 1998. *Language and History in the early Germanic world*, Cambridge: Cambridge University Press.

Lindow, John. 2001. *Norse mythology: a guide to the gods, heroes, rituals and beliefs*, Oxford: Oxford University Press.

Simek, Rudolf. 2000. *Dictionary of northern mythology*, trans. Angela Hall, 3rd edition, Cambridge: D.S. Brewer.

Celestial Light:
The Iconography of Apollon and Heru-Wer
by Samantha Lykeia Sanders

Yet light's divine presence has not yet come, when an impalpable glimmer suffuses the night, what waking men call wolf-light, they entered the harbor of Thynias, barren island, and stumbled ashore, exhausted by their grievous labors; and here there appeared before them Apollo, Leto's son .... Come, let us call this place the holy island of Dawntime Apollo, since here he revealed himself to us all, passing by at dawn. — **Argonautika** by Apollonios Rhodios, 669 & 686

This passage is an excellent illustration of the light of Apollon, associated with the sun as it may be, but not in this case regarded *as* the sun. Light flies before the rising sun led by dawn, and light suffuses the world as the sun travels along its path. Apollon bears light with him, so it is not surprising that he would be later associated strongly with the sun god Helios. However, the light that precedes the dawn is pointed out to have been the morning star visible in the pre-dawn, and which was considered completely separate from the evening star (http://history.nasa.gov/SP-424/ch1.htm).

The gathering and waning of light as it enters and leaves the sky can be associated with Apollon strongly, for a deity who presides over light

106

in the world would be equally linked with its absence, as well (just as the god was equated with both plague *and* healing).

This parallel can also be found in Egyptian mythology with Horus (or, Heru-Wer), where it is possible that the earliest divine image was that of a hawk in a barque. Geraldine Pinch in her book *Egyptian Mythology* remarks that it may have represented a planet or star traveling on the waterways across the sky. Wallis Budge in *Egyptian Heaven and Hell* describes the scene as the boat of Re enters the eastern horizon, and before him is Horus-Set, a combination of the dual/dueling forces of disease and darkness, and light. This powerful combination of Horus and Set strongly parallels the complex nature of Apollon.

This essay will demonstrate several areas of overlap and syncretism between Apollon (and the Roman Apollo) and Horus, such as their connections to the morning and evening stars; their conflation with the god of the sun; their role as the "light behind the light"; their role as gods of vengeance; and their association with the lion and the griffin. Such an examination allows for a deeper understanding of Apollon.

The Morning and Evening Stars

It is Horus-Set with his two bows, one in the darkness and one in the light, who comes into the sky before Re as Horus of the Dawn, the golden Horus. Horus has such strong associations with dawn time that he has the titles of Horemakhet (Horus of the Horizon) and Harmachis (Horus of the Two Horizons).

While the ancient Greeks saw the morning star as Apollon, and the evening star as Hermes, among the Egyptians the morning star was Set fleeing before the approaching light of Re, and the evening star represented the presence of Horus. But since, as already mentioned, Set and Horus were combined together in the company of the boat of Re then this is likely a case of mythical logic, of both/and, not either/or.

God(s) of the Sun

However; like Apollon in Greece, Horus, too, became confused and identified with the sun god within the Egyptian religion, gaining the title of Ra-Horakhty (Ra-Horus of the Double Horizon) as he is mentioned in *The Contendings of Horus and Set*. More frequently, though, both Apollon and Horus are individual deities distinct from the sun-god. The Romans who adopted Apollon into their religion rarely associated him with the sun. The only notable evidence of this association in early Roman literature occurs in the writings of Ovid, who was influenced by Greek philosophy, as well as in the philosophical writings of Cicero. However, this association was never very popular.

One of the most frequently used titles, even over and above the name Apollo, is that of Phoebus. The equivalent Roman title Lucifer (like the Lucina, a nocturnal light and light of birth epithet used for Diana, Hekate, and Iuno) is derived from the Latin word *lux*. Interestingly, his sister Diana was also associated with a wandering star (planet) as mentioned by Cicero in *On the Nature of the Gods*, and, given her epithet of Luciferia, it may have well been a relationship similar to that of Apollon and Hermes as the morning and evening star.

The Light Behind the Sun

In *A Summary of Pythagorean Theology*, John Opsopaus describes Apollon as the trans-mundane sun. That is, not the literal sun that governs the planets, but rather on a level between that and the heavenly Zeus. He is a light of logic and "rules the Ideas in the Empyrean Realm." Thus he could be explained as a light behind the sun. This would be remarkably similar to Horus, the celestial falcon whose wings span the sky at one thousand cubits; who banishes darkness when he opens his eyes, revealing the sun and the moon. He is not the sun, but the sun is within the scope of his essence and power as it filters down to humanity.

Horus takes on a great expanse of celestial light, for not only does he show himself in ways already mentioned, but he is also associated with other planets. The light of the planet Mars was the flight of Red Horus in the sky. Saturn, in turn, was Horus the Bull. Lastly, the planet Jupiter was Horus the Revealer of Secrets. In this last instance, we can equate Horus strongly with Apollon who used his oracles to speak to will of his father Zeus, but also served as a light that banished ignorance in favor of knowledge and logic, testifying to the power of the light to reveal the world to us.

The Light of Vengeance

However, in direct contrast Horus is also revealed at Letopolis as Horus the Not-Seeing, which may reference times of eclipse or any time that lacks visible light. This Khenty-en-irty (Eyeless Horus) is described by Pinch as a vengeful god who tortured the evil dead. Apollon, too, displays a vengeful character in myths in which insult is given to himself or his mother Leto, and in his grievances against faithless lovers. Concentration on Apollon's rule over logic, discovery, knowledge, and light, can lead to his role plague bringer and destroyer being overlooked. He is also Hekatos, the god who shoots from afar. And there, too, is Harwer/Haroeris (aka Horus) whose name is speculated to mean "Distant One," a god who can become a griffin (a combination of lion, serpent and falcon) to destroy the enemies of his father.

The Lion and the Griffin

In the Egyptian tale of *The Distant Goddess*, Thoth says that not even the mighty lion can escape slaughter by the griffin if he disobeys the laws of Re. The griffin is also a heraldic animal for Apollon, carrying him to the distant Hyperborean lands.

Interestingly, the lion — a ferocious animal often connected with powerful goddesses in mythology and familiar in modern astrology as the fiery Leo — is appropriately part of the iconography of both Horus and Apollon. Aside from being a component of the griffin, great lions stand roaring at Apollo's sacred site of Delos. In Egypt, the great Sphinx standing at Giza was recognized around 1500 BCE as Hor-em-akht (Horus in the Horizon), Bw-How (Place of Horus) and also as Ra-horakhty (Ra of Two Horizons). This would be quite appropriate considering that the lioness goddesses, associated with the sun eye, guarded the horizon as the sun rose above it.

Of course, it is amusing how many of the qualities of these gods have been remembered in popular culture through the ages, as the protective heraldic image of the fighting griffin, and in the astrological Leo, a sign associated directly with the sun as its planetary ruler.

Conclusion

Apollon is a complex god, honored across thousands of years and thousands of miles. While associated most strongly with light, this concept is nuanced, containing multiple meanings and levels. Exploring Apollon's similarities with Horus (and Horus-Set) allows for a deeper understanding of this complicated god.

Bibliography

Apollonios Rhodios, *The Argonautika* University of California Press (1997)

Budge, E.A. Wallis, *Egyptian Heaven and Hell.* Open Court Publishing Company (1905,1974)

Cicero, *The Nature of the Gods.* Penguin Classics (1972).

Pinch, Geraldine. *Egyptian Mythology: A Guide to Gods, Goddesses, and Traditions of Ancient Egypt.* Oxford Press (2002)

Fontenrose, Joseph E. *Apollo and Sol in the Latin Poets of the First Century BC.* Transactions and Proceedings of the American Philological Association. Vol 70 (1939) pp 439-455

Lyle, Jenson. The Story of the Sphinx (2007). Accessed 6/4/2007.

Simpson, William Kelly. The Contendings of Horus and Seth. Accessed 6/4/2007.

Took, Thalia. OGOD: Lucina (2004). Accessed 6/4/2007.

Opsopaus, John. A Summary of Pythagorean Theology (2002). Accessed 6/4/2007.

The Light of Apollon

by Amanda Artemisia Forrester

Phoibos [Apollon], of you even the swan sings
with clear voice to the beating of his wings,
as he alights upon the bank by the eddying river
            Peneios;
and of you the sweet-tongued minstrel,
holding his high-pitched lyre,
always sings both first and last. And so hail to you
            lord!
I seek your favour with my song.

    — *Homeric Hymn 21 to Apollon*

O Phoebus Apollon, divine musician, teacher
Who taught the melodious Muse her music, you
Who bathed in Xanthus' stream, beardless Agyieus,
Protector of the city,
Befriend me now and my Apulian Muse,
Phoebus Apollon who taught me the rules of the art
And gave me the name of poet.

    — Horace, *To Apollon*

Apollon is a God Who helps people to improve themselves. He encourages us to strive for the Hellenic virtue of *arete*, or excellence in all things, but especially in music, athletic fields, science, and philosophy. Apollon is the philosopher's God, and the inspirer of scientific inquiry. He is a punisher of injustice, yet also a redeemer and a purifier of miasma. Through His oracle at Delphi, He communicated the will of His father, Zeus, to the world. Apollon continues to bless us with strength and wisdom, and heals our sicknesses -- physical, mental, and spiritual.

Apollon is the twin brother of Artemis. He is called a Sun-God in many children's mythology books and high school classes, but He is much more. Apollon fulfills many functions. He is a God of oracles and prophecy, music and poetry, ritual and purification, plagues and healing, archery and hunting. He is also the God and protector of strangers and streets. One of Apollon's epithets is Paian, meaning "Healer." As well as being the God of Healing, Apollon is the father of Asklepios, the God of Medicine, who as a mortal was such a skilled healer he could raise the dead.

As Sun-God, Apollon represents not the sun itself (that is Helios), but the *effect* of the sun, the power and heat of it. Apollon is often shown with bow and arrows, the arrows being apt symbols for the rays of the sun. He can be gentle and beneficial, like the sun that sustains plants and causes fruits to ripen — but He does have a temper: the Sun can also burn. Apollon is the balance point between rationality and emotion, logic and temper, intellect and passion. He is the brightness of the educated mind, and He is the burning fire of senseless passion. He is both. Although occasionally prone to fits of temper, they are rarely without cause.

Apollon, like Athena, is patron of all the arts, but His main mode of expression is music. He is a companion of the Muses, the nine Goddesses Who inspire artists and writers of all kinds. While Athena is the *craftiness* of an artist, Apollon is the *passion* of the artist. Both Gods represent skill in the arts, but They exemplify different aspects of that skill. To be a good artist requires three things: passion for the arts, from Apollon; strategy and craftiness from Athena; and inspiration, from the Muses.

Some stories say that Apollon is the father of Orpheus, the greatest musician who ever lived and the founder of the Orphic Mysteries. Others say that Orpheus' mother was Kalliope, the Muse of Epic Poetry and the eldest Muse. They could not both be Orpheus's parents, as Orpheus was a mortal.

Apollon blesses us with artistic ability and athletic skill, justice and clear thought. He teaches us the Hellenic ideal of moderation and self-control. But we must remember that even moderation can be used in excess.

Apollon is portrayed as a handsome youth, an eternal teenager, with long uncut hair, usually tied up behind His head. His sacred animals are the crow (or raven in some sources)[1], which often acts as His messenger; the wolf[2]; and the dolphin[3]. Among these animals we cannot, at first, find a connection. One is a creature of air, another a creature of land, the last of sea. On this mystery Todd Jackson, the founder of a group devoted to the God called Kyklos Apollon[4], has this to say in his essay *On Apollon* "each [is] an eruption of intelligence within Nature; of intelligence as Nature's fruit, rather than as Nature's opposite[5]."

Swans[6], ethereal symbol of grace and transcendence, are sacred to Him, as well. One of His symbols is the tripod, upon which His priestess, the Pythia, sat while uttering her prophesy. His sacred number is seven, the day He was honored in the Athenian lunar calendar. In Alexandria He was

---

[1] *Hesiod. Catalogues of Women* Fragment 89, Pseudo-Apollodorus, *Bibliotheca* 3. 118, Pseudo-Hyginus. *Fabulae* 202

[2] Pausanias describes how a particular temple of Apollon in Athens was called the Lykeion, from the Greek word for wolf. (Pausanias. *Description of Greece*, 1. 19. 3). This is apparently quite common; there is also one is Argos (*Description of Greece* 2. 19. 3 - 8) and Argive (8. 46. 3).

[3] Suidas s.v. Delphinion

[4] Kyklos, from the Greek for circle. So Kyklos Apollon means, roughly, "Circle of Apollon".

[5] www.kyklosApollon.org/Apollon.htm

[6] Homeric Hymn 21 to Apollon

equated with the Egyptian God Horus[7].

Titles and Epithets of Apollon

Phoibos, "Bright", is the most commonly heard epithet of Apollon, so much so that He is often called Phoibos Apollon, or simply Phoibos, and all know it is to Him we are referring.

More titles refer to Him as related to light, such as Aiglêtos "The Shining," Leukatas, "of the Light," and Aigletes, "Radiant." Interestingly, none of these names overtly identify Him as a Sun-God or refer directly to the Sun.

Paian, "Healer," is another major aspect of Apollon. As such He has many titles of this sort. Acesius "Of Healing," Epicurius "Succouring" or "Helping," Boêdromios "Rescuer," and Iatros "Doctor." Apollon is Epikourios, "Helper" or "Ally." Alexikakos, "Averter of Evil/Harm," is in reference to His purification of miasma. Spodios, "Of the Ashes," which means the ashes on the altar after sacrifices were burnt, may also be related to His job as purifier.

Apollon is Mousêgetês, "Leader of Muses," and Kitharodos, "Singer to the Lyre." Aristaios, "Best," names Apollon as the God Who inspires excellence. Thearios means "Of the Oracle." He is called Daphnephoros "Bay-Bearer," mentioning His

---

[7] Plutarch. *On Isis and Osiris* 12, Eusebius of Caesarea. *Praeparatio Evangelica* 3.15, Herodotus 2.144, Diodorus Siculus 1.25

sacred plant which was burned in the temple of Delphi.

His rustic side is emphasized in His names Nomios, "Herdsman" or "Shepherd," Agraios, "Hunter/Of the Hunt," and Hekatos, "Shooter from Afar." Lukeios "of the Wolf," names one of His sacred animals, as does Delphinios, "Of the Dolphins."

Apollon, the God of the *ephebe*, is called Hersos, meaning "New Born" or "Divine Child," and Kourotrophos, "Protector of Youth." He was called Genetor, meaning "Begetter" and "Ancestor," and Patrôios "Of the Fathers" or "Ancestral," because through Him, several tribes and cities came to be. It was His son Ion who founded the great Ionian tribe.

He is called Amazonios "Of the Amazons" because, after Artemis and Ares, He was believed to be one of the patron Gods of the Amazons. Hyperborean, "of the Far North," refers to the obscure myth that Apollon resides in Delphi for only half the year. In the winter Dionysos takes over Delphi, and Apollon retreats to the mythical northern land of Hyperborea.

Apollon and Pytho
When Leto wandered the earth before Apollon and His sister Artemis were born, seeking in vain a kingdom that would allow Her to give birth, Hera sent a great dragon called Pytho, or Python, to pursue poor pregnant Leto. Bad enough

118

that everyone was too afraid of Hera's wrath to take Her in; Leto also had to outrun a monster intent on destroying Her.

After Apollon's birth He was determined to hunt down the monster that had pursued His mother and who had tried to kill Him and His sister while still in the womb. He was only four days old, but He pursued Python to its lair at Delphi. It was a great battle, but Apollon won, piercing the dragon with His arrows, and leaving the beast to rot in the sun. So He earned the title Pythios, "Of the Python." But to be purified of the killing of Pytho Apollon had to serve a mortal as his slave for a "great year," a period of eight to nine years. Some people believed that it was not just Apollon who killed Pytho, but that his sister Artemis hunted the beast with Him[8], but She apparently did not share in His penance.

So Apollon was given to King Admetos to serve as a slave. This was in the hills of Thessaly, and Karl Kerenyi refers to it as Apollon's "pastoral time." Apollon became very fond of His master. He helped Admetos to win His wife, Alkestis. Further, Kerenyi states that "when the time came for the King to die, Apollon saves him by making the Moirai drunk. When Death came for Admetos a second time, Alkestis went in place of her husband, but was later brought back by Herakles[9]." I find this

8   Pausanias. *Description of Greece* 2. 7. 7 - 9

9   Kerenyi, Karl. *The Gods of the Greeks*. Thames and Hudson. 1951. London.

tale extremely interesting. These actions seem to fit more with the Trickster Hermes then with the somber and sometimes severe philosopher's God. It tells us that there is more to Apollon then simply the champion of moderation and rational thought.

Delphi, The Navel of the World

After Apollon was freed from His period of bondage, He returned to Delphi, the site of His defeat of Pytho. Apollon went about establishing His cult in Delphi. There was a ship of men sailing from Krete on their way to mainland Greece. Apollon is said to have abducted these men and bought them to Delphi to serve as His priests. This is interesting, as it establishes early on a connection to Krete, the home of the Minoan civilization.

Technically the Minoans were not Greek, although they could be called a precursor to Greek culture. They were certainly an influence. The Deities Whose mythology likely was influenced the most by Minoan religion are Demeter and Her daughter Persephone, Rhea, Hera and Dionysos, and to some extent Athena. This mythic detail, however, implies that Apollon may have come from Krete, as well.

Although the name of Delphi may be pre-Greek, it was connected with the Greek word *delphys*, "womb." Delphi was a sacred site connected to prophecy long before Apollon claimed it.

This venerable oracular site, where from ancient times the sacrality and the powers of Mother Earth were manifested, received a new religious orientation under the reign of Apollon[10].

It was from this temple at Delphi that Apollon's priestess, the Pythia, issued her world-famous oracles. People from all over the Hellenic world would travel to Delphi to ask the Pythia questions. A goat would be sacrificed before the temple, and the supplicant would then be ushered in. The Pythia descended into a chamber under the temple called the *adyton*, where the prophecy would take place. She was inspired by the God in a trance-like state, and often what she said would sound like gibberish and the priests would have to step in and interpret.

Mircea Eliade, the author of the three volume *A History of Religious Ideas*, seems confused as how these altered states were brought on, since there are no signs of any type of, as he puts it, "intoxicating properties." Scholars are usually quick to assume that any accounts of trance or other "unusual" experiences are due to some type of hallucinogen. Of course, they never consider that it might come from an actual spiritual experience.

---

[10] Eliade, Mircea. *A History of Religious Ideas: Volume One – From the Stone Age to the Eleusinian Mysteries.* Translated by Willard R. Trask, University of Chicago Press, 1978. Page 271.

The laurel leaves that she chewed, fumigations with laurel, the water from the spring Cassotis that she drank have no intoxicating properties and do not explain the trance. According to tradition, her oracular tripod was placed over a cleft (*chasma*) in the ground from which vapors with supernatural virtues rose. Excavations, however, have brought to light neither a fissure in the ground nor the cavern into which the Pythia descended (but it may be admitted that they may have disappeared as the result of earthquakes). The conclusion has been reached, a little too quickly, that the whole apparatus – *chasma* with vapors, descent of the Pythia into the corridor (the *adyton*) – is a comparatively recent mythical image. Yet the *adyton* existed, and, as Marie Delcourt shows (*L'oracle de Delphes*, pp. 227 ff.), the antiquity and telluric structure of Delphi implied a ritual "descent" into the underground regions[11].

In the Greek belief, Delphi was so important, so sacred, that it was considered the navel, or center, of the world. It was at Delphi that

[11] Eliade, Mircea. *A History of Religious Ideas: Volume One – From the Stone Age to the Eleusinian Mysteries.* Translated by Willard R. Trask, University of Chicago Press, 1978. Page 272.

Apollon handed down His maxims to the Seven Sages, the guide to the Hellenic way of life.

Apollon and Daphne
Or, How Apollon Gained His Sacred Tree

It starts when Apollon foolishly makes fun of Eros, God of Love and son of Aphrodite, when He was aiming at someone with His bow and arrow. "Why is such a little boy so concerned with powerful weapons? Such weapons are suitable only for me. I am the one who is able to give sure wounds to wild animals, my enemies. See to it that you are content to kindle the little flames of love with your torch and do not try to claim a skill for which I am famous."

Eros just smiled enigmatically and flew away. He waited several days until a perfect opportunity presented itself. Apollon was walking in the countryside when His eyes fell upon a beautiful young nymph, a daughter of the River-God Peneus, who was called Daphne. Eros quickly pierced Apollon's heart with a gold-tipped arrow, causing love; but Daphne He shot with an iron (or lead)-tipped one, causing instant hatred and revolution. Apollon, smote with the consuming passion and love of Eros, ran after the nymph, determined to seduce her and make her His. Daphne, however, acting on the effect of Eros's iron arrow, was no less determined *not* to become Apollon's lover.

She ran away. But running away only made

123

her more beautiful; her windswept hair and flushed cheeks made her all the more alluring, and we all know that we often want the one thing we can't have.

Apollon sprinted after her. The nymph was swift of feet, but Apollon was a runner of great skill. However, he did not run as fast as he could have. He did not want to catch her, He wanted her to stop of her own free will. He called ahead to her (and I am abbreviating this!) "I am not pursuing you as an enemy…It is love that is the reason for my pursuit. I am not a shepherd or wild man of the mountains; I am son of Zeus…[12]" He was trying to impress her, which didn't work. She still ran.

When Daphne was so fatigued that she could barely run anymore, she saw at last the water of the River Peneus, and cried out to her father to help her, asking him to destroy her beauty so that no male would be interested in her. As Ovid puts it:

> She had hardly finished her prayer when a heavy numbness filled her limbs, and her soft body encircled by thin bark, her hair changed to leaves, her arms to branches. Her feet, just a moment ago too swift, clung to the ground in dull roots, and her head turned into a treetop. Her beauty alone remained

---

[12] For Apollon's full speech, see *Classical Gods and Heroes: Myths as Told by the Ancient Authors*, pg. 53

unchanged[13].

Apollon stilled loved her, even in tree shape. He said to her "Since you cannot be my wife, you will be my tree. My hair, my lyre, my quiver will always bear you, O laurel, as adornment…And as my head is always young with uncut locks, may you always keep the beauty of your leaves everlasting green."

And ever since the laurel tree has been considered to be sacred to Apollon. Unsurprisingly, Daphne means 'laurel' or 'bay tree' in Greek.

Apollon and the Death of Youth

Apollon had many lovers; nymphs, mortal women, and mortal men. One such lover was Hyacinthus, a youth of Sparta, some say the Prince of Sparta himself. His interests included hunting, music, and athletics. He must have been an exceptional young man to draw Apollon's attention, the God of all three of those things.

But Zephyros, the West Wind, had also fallen in love with him. Hyacinthus chose Apollon, however, and Zephyros was hurt, jealous, and angry. One day while Apollon and Hyacinthus were playing quoits, a discus game, the wind ripped the discus out of the God's hand and directed it at

---

[13] Ovid. *Metamorphoses*. 1. 452

Hyacinthus[14]. The boy was hit hard in the head, a fatal wound. Apollon ran to his love, blaming Himself for not being more careful with the fragile human. He held the body of His mortal lover and wept. Apollon turned him into a hyacinth, a beautiful flower that blooms in the spring. The petals quickly wither and die, a symbol of youth cut tragically short. Some say that Apollon also took Hyacinthus's spirit to Olympos to remain His companion, even in death.

There are many more examples with other youths whose tales end in premature death, such as the young Cyparissus. Poor Apollon seems to be singularly unlucky in love. Apollon rules over the *ephebe*, or the coming of age time when Greek boys began to become men.

Stereotypical Greek love, that is, the love between a man and a youth, is looked down upon today. Many people in modern societies detest the idea and see it as no different from child abuse. Greeks did not condone child abuse; sexual relations with anyone under the age of twelve was strictly punished. Girls in Athens were married not long after they began to menstruate, often at around thirteen or fourteen years of age. Boys became youths at the onset of puberty. They became

---

[14] It should be noted that this was an uncharacteristic act for Zephyros, who is usually the mildest and gentlest of the Winds. In fact, some insist that Hyacinthus' death was purely accidental, brought on by Apollon's superhuman strength.

*ephebe*s, a concept similar to our idea of teenager, but with some differences. An ephebe was no longer a child, and not as protected sexually as our teenagers often are, but he still had to learn what it meant to be a man.

The adult was called the *erastes*, which means "lover," and the youth was *eromenos*, "the beloved." It was the job of the *erastes* to teach the *eromenos* how to be a responsible Greek citizen. He took his youthful lover to symposiums to learn philosophy and ethics, discipline and how to behave, taught him about legislation and the affairs of the city, and inducted him into public life. The relationship only lasted through the *eromenos'* teenage years, and when he became a man it typically ended.

An educated adult was charged with transmitting his knowledge and experience to an adolescent, and with helping him become a responsible citizen. The adult, in return, admired and enjoyed the beauty, strength, and vigor of the youth. A two-way communication was thus created for the benefit of both. The concept that strength, courage, knowledge, and virtue can pass down from the older and more experienced to the younger and inexperienced, but also that the vigor of the young can be conveyed to the older through a close relationship, is primordial. ... It is thus clear, that pederasty was an institution of noble and high ideals. … And that's what differentiates it from any similar institution found in any other civilization[15].

As the God ruling over the time of the *ephebe*, it is appropriate that Apollon is depicted in loving relationship with many youths. Further, all of Apollon's love affairs with youths ended in death, with His beloved being wrenched away from Him. I'm sure that is what it may have felt like to many an *erastes* when the *ephebe* grew to manhood, and the couple — per the dictates of Athenian culture —had to give up the relationship. Growing to adulthood was not just the death of childhood, but the death of a romantic relationship.

Apollon and Spiritual Experience

Apollon in myth and tragedy had a habit of chasing down women and carrying them off, a plot line that can be quite disturbing to the modern feminist reader. Besides His pursuit of Daphne, and also the "carrying off[16]" or "seizing[17]" of the Thessalonian princess Kyrene, and the forcing of Kreousa, the mother of Ion, there are others. Many

---

[15] Vrissimtzis, Nikos A. *Love, Sex and Marriage in Ancient Greece: A Guide to the Private life of the Ancient Greeks.* 1997. Greece. Pg 73.

[16] Apollonius Rhodius. *Argonautica* 2. 498

[17] Pindar. *Pythian Ode* 9. 6

of the words used in the original texts are ambiguous, so that we cannot be sure whether the women involved were willing participants or not. Sadly, this is not unusual for the writing of the time.

Kala Trobe, author of *Invoke the Gods: Exploring the Power of Male Archetypes,* meditates on this dichotomy of Apollon the God of healing and moderation, and His sometimes savage temper and possibly violent pursuit of women.

> We are faced with the fact that either those who participated in the genesis of Apollon's legends did not believe such actions to be wrong ... or that the events described were intended, along with similar scenarios enacted by Zeus and Pluto, to be taken as allegories. If such is the case, they may be interpreted as unsought infusions of elevated thought; sudden inspirations that leave the recipient bemused as to how to cope with the issue. Mystics of many religions undergo experiences of divine communication, only to find themselves "abandoned" when the effect wears off and they are left with the harsh realities of the solid world. Genius undergoes a similar fate, being incompatible with mundane reality. It would be possible to attribute the shame and bitterness of mythical Grecian women abandoned by the gods to the effects of mystical aftermath -– the "Why hast thou

forsaken me?" principle. Just as the oracular Delphic Pythia might find her mouth "torn" by Apollon, so might a divine infusion "tear" the perceptions of the devotee. Divinity is too vast for the common experience[18].

Reading Trobe's interpretation stuck a tone within me. It was powerful experiences with Athena as a child that lead me to Hellenismos. It was She, and Artemis, that nursed me through my painful and angst-filled teenage years. Through the darkness of my parents' yearlong custody battle, through the senseless bullying and religious persecution I suffered in high school, it was my Gods Who sustained me. The presence of Athena and Artemis in my life was near-constant. They were my light, my loves, my life.

Years later, the dark mists of Erebos receded and my life stabilized. I moved out from my father's house and began to make my way in the world. I fell in love with a good and decent man and I began to truly enjoy my life for the first time in quite a while.

But although the quality of my life overall had vastly improved, I began to go through a spiritual crisis. It felt as if the Gods had withdrawn

---

[18] Trobe, Kala. *Invoke the Gods: Exploring the Power of Male Archetypes.* Llewellyn Publications. 2001. St. Paul, MN.

from my life. I was used to feeling Athena always near, hovering over my shoulder, as with Odysseus in Homer's *Odyssey*. But now I no longer felt Her presence constantly. I worried that perhaps Athena had abandoned me because I was no longer a virgin. I began to doubt whether Athena was still my patron, or if She had ever been at all.

It is now known that even Mother Theresa had moments where she doubted the existence of God. She had a powerful and transformative mystic experience when she was young that drove her to serve her God in Calcutta. But after an experience like that, mundane existence can be difficult, even painful.

But I came to understand that I did not need the Gods with me in every waking step anymore. Athena and Artemis had nurtured me, accepted me as I was, and helped me through one of the most difficult periods of my life. I have no doubt that without Them, I would have taken my own life while still in high school. But I was completely dependent upon Them, and the Gods want willing worshipers, not slaves who can't live without them. They withdrew for a time, until I learned to survive on my own. I struggled with myself and with Them, but I would not give up my faith. I already knew what beauty the Gods could bring into my life. I just had to learn to relate to Them in a more healthy manner.

I began to conduct more rituals. Through high school, I did not do many rituals. I did some;

but Athena and Artemis were always by my side, I had no need to call for Them. For the first three or so years after I had stumbled onto Paganism, I thought belief was enough. But true worship is more than belief, more than warm fuzzy thoughts. As I began to bring my faith and my love for the Gods into the physical world, through action in ritual, through prayers spoken aloud, through offerings to Them on Their shrines, I began to feel Them in my life once again.

I had learned a valuable lesson of Hellenic Paganism: that ours in a religion of practice. It is not enough to simply believe in the Gods in your heart, you must show it to Them. It is not so strange an idea. After all, you must *show* your partner or your children that you love them, not just *say* that you do. Otherwise, they will soon begin to doubt your devotion. Actions speak louder than words.

It is the same with our Gods. We must make time for Them, even if it is only a little. The rituals and prayers do not have to be grand, theatric productions; meditating in front of Their altars, hands uplifted, for five minutes a day is a powerful and effective way to bring Them into our daily lives.

We give the Gods offerings to show our appreciation and respect. Would you remain friends for long with someone who only wanted to see you when they needed something? Of course not. Eventually, your kindness would run out. Nobody likes to be used. Similarly we must not fall into the trap of approaching the Gods only when we want something. It is easy to do, but we must guard against it. We must share our happy times with the Gods, as well as our needy pangs and our moments of despair, if we are to truly call Them our friends.

The Contest of Apollon and Marsyas

As God of Music and Poetry, Apollon's chosen instrument was the lyre, which had been made by His brother Hermes. Hermes had invented a three-stringed lyre, and Apollon had added four more strings to it, creating an even more perfect, harmonious sound.

Marsyas is usually said to have been a Satyr, although some say he was a Sileni. Both in mythology and art, there is confusion between Satyrs and Sileni, as they are closely related. Some ancient authors go so far as to say that the Sileni are the elder Satyrs, the first generation. However, it should be noted that there are physical differences between the two which suggest that they are two different races. Satyrs have the torso and face of a human male, but the legs, tail, and horns of a goat. Sileni have the tail and sometimes the ears of a horse, pug noses, and sometimes a balding head. There is argument, even among the ancients, as to whether the Satyrs and Sileni are immortal or merely extremely long lived. The Sileni are also sometimes called the Ipotane.

Whatever his race, Marsyas was an upstart musician. His instrument was a double flute, and his skill was such that he came to have on inflated opinion of himself. He became a huge braggart. He went so far as to challenge Apollon to a contest of music, and considering that Apollon is the God of Music, this was an extremely arrogant move. And as I have said before, if there is anything the Gods hate, it's having the conceit and pride to place ourselves on the same level as the Divine.

Apollon could not possibly refuse, as to do so would mean that Marsyas could say that He was afraid to lose. He accepted the challenge. Some say that the Muses were the Judges; some say it was King Midas of Phrygia. This is the same King Midas who received the Golden Touch from Dionysos, and was later appointed as one of the three Judges of the Underworld. Some say that Tmolus, father of Omphale (mistress of Herakles), was co-judge of the contest.

Apollon started the contest by playing a beautiful, heavenly tune on His trusty lyre. Marsyas followed it up with a composition that was nearly as impressive as Apollon's. Some say that Apollon flipped His lyre upside down and played another beautiful song that way and He won because you can't play a double flute backwards, for obvious reasons. Others say that Apollon won because He sang as well as played the lyre. Marsyas protested, saying that it was an instrument contest not a singing contest. Apollon responded by saying that, as Marsyas blew into the pipes, he was doing almost the same thing himself.

After comparing their skills again, Tmolus gave the victory to Apollon, and everyone attending agreed with Tmolus' judgment. But Midas thought that Marsyas should have been the winner. Perhaps he believed that Apollon was cheating, perhaps he just preferred flute music to that of the lyre. Apollon declared "You will have ears to match the mind you have in judging" and King Midas' ears changed from human to that of an ass. Some say that Apollon flayed Marsyas alive, which is definitely a harsher punishment! Fit me for some ass' ears, please!

As for Midas, he was incredibly embarrassed about his new donkey ears, which he took to hiding under a large purple turban. Only his barber knew about the new part of Midas's anatomy, and he was sworn to secrecy. The barber was just itching to tell someone, anyone. He did not want to betray his King, however. He had the juiciest piece of gossip in all Phrygia, and he couldn't tell a soul!

For a long time he kept the secret, even though he longed to tell someone. One day he just can't stand it anymore. So the barber went out into a meadow and dug a tiny little hole in the dirt and whispered into it "King Midas has ass' ears." He then buried the hole and went back to town feeling much better.

A few weeks later, a bunch of weeds had grown up on that exact spot where the barber dug the hole. The reeds sighed softly into the wind

"King Midas has ass' ears. King Midas has ass' ears." Somebody overheard and ran to town to tell everyone. Soon Midas was the laughing stock of Phrygia.

This story can be seen as a cautionary tale showing us to be careful what we say even when we think we are alone; after all, even the walls (or the ground) have ears.

Asklepios the Physician

Great Asklepios, skilled to heal mankind,
all-ruling Paian, and physician kind;
whose arts medicinal can alone assuage
diseases dire, and stop their dreadful rage.
Strong, lenient God, regard my suppliant prayer,
bring gentle health, adorned with lovely hair;
convey the means of mitigating pain,
and raging deadly pestilence restrain.
O power all-flourishing, abundant, bright,
Apollon's honoured offspring, God of light;
husband of blameless Hygeia (Health),
the constant foe of dread disease, the minister of
*   woe:*
come, blessed saviour, human health defend,
and to the mortal life afford a prosperous end.

— *Orphic Hymn* 67 to Asclepius

Apollon is the God of Healing, and the father of the God of Medicine, Asklepios. The

Romans spelled his name as Aesculapius, or Asclepius. The last one is the spelling you will usually see. Asklepios' symbol is a tall staff with one snake curled around it. His temples often kept snakes, cared for by the priestesses, and they were believed to be a form of Asklepios on earth. Asklepios was equated by Alexandrian Greeks with the Egyptian Physician-God Imhotep and is thought by some modern Hellenes to be an aspect of Apollon Himself. Some might go so far as to consider him an avatar, or mortal incarnation of the God, much as Krishna is considered by Hindus to be an avatar of Vishnu. Either way, I prefer to treat Asklepios as a separate entity from Apollon.

Asklepios began life as mortal. Apollon fell in love with a beautiful maiden named Koronis, the daughter of the Thessalonian horse-breeder Phlegyas. Koronis became His lover, but He was almost never around because He had to spend so much time tending to his Godly duties.

The girl was lonely, and she took Iskhys of Elatos as a lover. The pair tried to keep their affair a secret, but they were seen by a raven, one of Apollon's sacred animals. Now, at this time, ravens were beautiful birds with snow-white feathers. They were still as chatty as today. The raven immediately flew to Delphi, declaring the unfortunate news to Apollon. Apollon had already known this in His heart, but was in denial. The harsh words from the raven were the straw that broke the camel's back. In a jealous rage, Apollon grabbed His bow and shot her through the heart[19]. Before she died, she was able to gasp out "Our child."

Apollon was consumed with guilt and grief. What had He done? How could He had acted so rashly, egged on by gossip from a bird? His grief turned to anger, which He directed at the raven: henceforth, all ravens have had feathers as black as night. Another version says that it was Apollon's twin sister Artemis who killed Koronis for her infidelity[20]. Artemis values purity and loyalty, and as a sister myself, I understand the urge to punish the one who wrongs your sibling.

As for Koronis, the villagers of Thessaly were already beginning to burn her body on a funeral pyre. Apollon reached out and snatched the baby boy from his mother's womb. He gave that boy, named Asklepios, to be raised by Kheiron, the wise immortal centaur[21].

Asklepios grew to become a wise doctor, a physician who could cure any ill. He married a woman by the name of Epione, who bore him two sons, Makhaon and Podalirius, who in Homer's *Iliad* follow in their father's footsteps to become

---

[19] Pseudo-Hyginus. *Fabulae* 202,

[20] Pindar. *Pythian Ode* 3. 5, Pausanias. *Description of Greece* 2. 26. 1 - 7

[21] Pseudo-Apollondorus. *Bibliotheca* 3. 118, Pindar. *Nemean Ode* 3. 51

physicians[22].

Asklepios was famed for his skill and loved by all. Edith Hamilton, in her *Mythology*, called him a universal benefactor[23]. Asklepios became not only a favorite of his father Apollon, but also of the wise Goddess Athena. It was Athena Who gifted Asklepios with two vials of blood from the dead Medousa[24], one from the right side, which could cure any ailment and even raise the dead, and one from the left, deadlier then any poison.

Asklepios brought many people back from the brink of death, and using the vials of Medousa's blood even raised the dead. This did not sit well with Hades, Lord of the Underworld. He began to complain to Zeus that His kingdom was being robbed of its rightful inhabitants. He added that Asklepios would begin to think himself a God, deciding who lived and who died. Zeus agreed, and killed Asklepios with a thunderbolt[25]. Pindar and several others said that it was not Hades who convinced Zeus to kill Asklepios, but that Zeus was

---

[22] Homer. *Iliad* 4. 193 & 217, Homer. *Iliad* 11. 518, Pseudo-Hyginus. *Fabulae* 97, Diodorus Siculus. *Library of History* 4. 71. 3

[23] Hailton, Edith. *Mythology: Timeless Tales of Gods and Heroes*. Warner Books. 1969. New York. Pg 294.

[24] Pseudo-Apollondorus. *Bibliotheca* 3. 121,

[25] Hesiod. *Catalogues of Women* Fragment 90,

offended when Asklepios violated his sacred oath and was toke a bribe to bring back a rich man[26]. By another tale, Artemis asked Asklepios to bring back Her devotee Hippolytus when he died through the machinations of Aphrodite[27].

Apollon was outraged at the death of his son, when he had merely been a good and compassionate doctor. Athena was also displeased. The people, who had loved Asklepios deeply, were angry with the Gods. So Zeus placed him in the sky as the constellation Ophiochos, the "Serpent Holder." Apollon and Athena convinced Zeus to deify Asklepios as well. As a God, there was no impropriety in raising the dead. Asklepios' wife Epione became the Goddess of Soothing and Comfort. After they ascended to Olympos, Asklepios and Epione had five immortal daughters, all related to the field of health and medicine. The eldest and most famous of the five was Hygeia[28], Goddess of health. Her sisters were Iaso[29], whose name means "Healer", the Goddess of recovery;

---

[26] Pindar, *Pythian Ode* 3. 54, Stesichorus, Fragment 147 , Plato. *Republic* 408b

[27] Philodemus, *On Piety,* Greek Lyric IV Stesichorus Frag 147 & Cinesias Frag 774

[28] Licymnius. Fragment 769, Apuleius. *The Golden Ass* 10. 25, Orphic Hymn 68 *to Hygeia*, Aeschylus. *Agamemnon* 1001, Euenus. Fragment 6

[29] Aristophanes. *Plutus* 701, Suidas s.v. Epione,

Aigle[30], "Radiance", the Goddess of the radiance of good health; Panakeia[31], "All-Cures", the Goddess of cures and medicines; and Akeso[32], the Goddess of healing and curing. While Her sister Panakeia represented the medicine itself, such as healing ointments and herbs, Akeso was a personification of the healing process. Greek mythology being what it is, in some cases Hygeia was said to be Asklepios' wife, not his daughter, as evidenced by the Orphic hymn that begins this section.

Asklepios became a popular God through the Greek and Roman world, perhaps because he began as a mortal, and knows the pain of human suffering in ways that his father Apollon cannot. His most sacred sanctuary was in Epidaurus, situated in the northeastern Peloponnese, and he is often referred to as the Epidaurian. His sacred animal is the cock or rooster, the animal typically sacrificed by those seeking a cure to an illness.

His cult became very popular during the 300s BCE. The sick would make pilgrimages to his cult centers in Epidaurus and elsewhere seeking healing. His cult centers had schools of medicine as well as temples. In those days, the scientific and the

---

[30] Greek Lyric V Anonymous, Fragment 939 (Inscription from Erythrai)

[31] Pausanias. *Description of Greece* 1. 34. 3,

[32] Suidas s.v. Epione

religious aspects of healing were not separated, so that doctors would prescribe the "real" treatment as well as recommending a certain sacrifice or prayer. Frances Bernstein, the author of *Classical Living: Reconnecting with the Rituals of Ancient Rome*, comments on the centers of Asklepios and Salus, the Roman Hygeia.

> The ancient healing shrines were not unlike our modern spas, except that first and foremost they were religious centers, sites of holistic healing and mind/body work under the power of the god and goddess where all aspects of the patient were treated. We can recapture the sage advice offered by Aesculapius and Salus. Ancient healing shrines were usually located in quiet valleys or sites away from a large city. Patients seeking cures from a variety of ailments, from baldness to lameness and disease, often stayed for months. The shrines were staffed with priests, priestesses, and attendants to guide patients through the cure. Diet was supervised and exercise such as walking, games, and sports was encouraged. As mental stimulation was considered important for a well-balanced life, the shrines contained libraries where philosophers and teachers lectured. Since drama, poetry, and music had a healing and cathartic effect upon patients, the larger shrines had theaters for

performances[33].

And his temples were as far flung as Trikkus in Thessaly, which appears to be the oldest. It was from the Isle of Kos, the site of another prominent temple to Asklepios, that Hippocrates hailed. The legendary Hippocrates was said to be a descendant of Asklepios. Doctors today still swear his Hippocratic Oath to do no harm. The original oath began with "I swear by Apollon the Physician and by Asklepios and by Hygeia and Panakeia and by all the gods and goddesses, that, according to my ability and judgment, I will keep this Oath and this stipulation …."

The primary practice of Asklepios' cult was dream incubation. The supplicant, after going through various rituals, would sleep in the temple. Often there would be a pit dug into the soil, in which the patient would sleep. Many times sacred (non-venomous) snakes who lived in the temple would be released to crawl over the sleeping supplicant. Asklepios was believed to visit the sleeper in his/her dreams, often giving the patient a remedy. If Asklepios did not explicitly state what would cure the supplicant, then the Priests would attempt to interpret the symbolism of the dreams.

---

[33] Bernstein, Frances. *Classical Living: Reconnecting with the Rituals of Ancient Rome.* HarperCollins Publishers. 2000. Pg 25.

Offerings to Apollon

Images of His sacred animals — crows, wolves, dolphins or swans — are good offerings, as always. As a God of art, it would be especially appropriate to draw or paint images of these animals or shape them from clay yourself.

Apollon's sacred plant of laurel was frequently burned in His temples. You can find whole bay leaves in the cooking aisle of most supermarkets alongside the other spices. Besides laurel leaves, frankincense and amber resin make lovely incense offerings. Sunflowers and hyacinths, the sacred plants of Apollon, are also appropriate gifts and will bring life to His altar as well.

Libations of honey and wine are always appropriate. Clear white wine aptly symbolizes His clear mind much better then red, in my completely personal opinion.

The best way to honor Apollon is to strive for excellence in all areas of your life. Exercise and try to live a healthy life. Study a subject that appeals to you. Read the philosophers, both classical philosophers and ones from later periods.

Support those in the medical profession. Donate to cancer or AIDS research and treatment. Volunteer at a nursing home or hospice. Visit the sick.

Keep your word. Be responsible. Live your principals, and strive for excellence. Take up some kind of art, especially singing or playing an instrument like a guitar or violin. Go to art shows and museums and support local artists.

*[Note: Excerpted from the author's forthcoming book, **Journey to Olympos: A Modern Spiritual Odyssey**.]*

Tales

Phoebus Apollo and the Hours
by Georg Friedrich Kersting

The Blue Bird and the Raven

by Rebecca Buchanan

"It jumped."

Sulian's low voice rumbled through the lab. The mice in their plexisteel habitat along the far wall squeaked and jumped, their tiny voices suddenly loud as conversations around the lab stumbled to a halt. Ferelith stilled, her breath catching. Across the table, Tsula let loose with a string of Cherokee oaths, snarling. Her dark copper skin took on a yellowish hue through the holomatrix that spun slowly in the air. Ferelith carefully set down her tablet, rolling the stylus between her fingers. She cleared her throat. "When?"

"Rumored yesterday. Blood work just came in at 0600, local." There was a buzzy snap as the com link fought through solar interference. " — *pound A."*

Ferelith leaned forward in her chair. "Say that again, Sulian?"

Another buzz, followed by a long hiss, then Sulian's clear voice. *"Better? Hear me again?"*

"Yes. Confirmation at 0600?"

Tsula reached across the table to grab the tablet, the holomatrix smearing across her arm, then sliding back into the figure of a complex filovirus as she hunched down in her own chair.

"Affirmative, at Ag Compound Alpha. Tillie came down with a fever at about 2330 hours,

local." There was a long pause. *"She started hemorrhaging at 0300. We're manufacturing plasma for her as fast as we can, but we've only got the one chamber and it can only produce one liter every three hours."* Another pause. *"Kiel — her son — he's got a fever now, too."*

Ferelith threw down the stylus and dug the heels of her hands into her eyes. "It accelerated. When it jumped the species barrier, the incubation period shortened."

"Yeah," Tsula grunted, poking at the tablet. Gianna quietly moved up beside her to peer over her shoulder, riot of brown curls pulled into a tight bun. The holomatrix quivered and then shattered, the long strand of the filovirus pulling away from its protein and lipid envelopes. The triple layers spun leisurely, their strange, alien proteins glowing green and purple and yellow.

Ferelith dropped her hands and pushed herself straighter in her chair. "Isolation and quarantine measures have been taken?"

"As soon as Tillie exhibited symptoms, yes. Alpha only has a two-bed clinic. It's a small facility, only five families and ten thousand head. It's fairly remote, too; three hours by shuttle to Eidsvoll across the Stig River."

"Alpha," Tsula interrupted. She frowned across the table at Ferelith. "Was it the first agricultural center established on Gefjun after terraformation?"

149

Another staticky hiss. *" — was. Is that significant?"*

"Mm, maybe," Tsula answered, followed by more poking. "Beam us the relevant medical files."

Ferelith rolled her eyes, adding a "Please" out loud. Gianna snickered.

There might have been a slight smile in Sulian's response. *"Already sent. Data packet should pop up any second — intact, hopefully. Counting the hours until you folks get here."*

"Thirty hours, weather permitting. Stay close to your com, and we'll keep working. Take care, Suli."

"I will. Blessings of Eir upon you, Feri. And Tsula."

"Erh." Poke, poke, poke.

The com link cut off with an audible snap. Ferelith tapped the intra-ship link embedded in her earlobe. "Doctor Henry to Com."

"Com, this is Tikahche." Her voice was soft and calm, efficient.

Wish I could be that calm. "Unole, a data packet is coming in from Gefjun. Could you please beam a copy back to the Iduny Med Temple, and get ready to bring them in on conference?"

"Affirmative, Ferelith. Standing by."

"Thank you." She tapped her earlobe again. "All personnel, please report to the lab."

***

Thirteen hours later, Ferelith stumbled into her tiny quarters and fell face-first into her bunk. She awkwardly pried off her shoes with her toes and closed her eyes, nose pressed deep into her pillow. Beneath the antiseptic smell of the *Ka-la-nu*'s automated laundry lay a faint hint of marglóð. She pressed her nose deeper and inhaled again.

Hyacinth plants — smuggled or accidentally transported — had integrated themselves into the native biosphere and taken to the slightly acidic soil of Iduny like fragrant weeds, adapting and evolving until they bore little resemblance to their Terran ancestors. Towering a good meter into the air, with thick petals that ranged from searing pink to icy blue, the flowers produced marglóð, a multilayered fragrance which was Iduny's only agricultural export.

Emphasis on *only*.

She inhaled again, deeper, drowning in the scent. Her body relaxed, at least a little, mind wandering back to childhood hours spent in her mother's perfume studio, telling stories about Gods and heroes and queens while extracting the essential oils, carefully measuring and remeasuring the marglóð and other ingredients. The small hand-made batches, never the same formula twice, were popular with both locals and pilgrims to the nearby temples of Freyja, Bragi, Aphrodite, and Apollo.

She rolled onto her back. Her mother had never understood why Ferelith went into epidemiology. Crafting perfume was an act of beauty, grace. Disease was … ugly; wretched.

Her mother was right. Disease *was* ugly. It was painful, messy, dehumanizing. Ten years of traveling from one viral hotspot to another around the system and beyond, and she had seen everything from a mutant strain of leprosy to an aerosolized aphthovirus to a vaccine-resistant poliovirus.

She turned her head, gaze settling on the small wall shrine to Apollo. The beautiful ivory statue of the God, crowned and cloaked in gold, had been a gift from a favorite instructor upon her graduation from medical school. A bundle of dried laurel leaves. A crow feather, picked up on her pilgrimage to Delphi. A phial of Essence of Light, made by her mother for her, only her.

A bit of beauty to take with you, she had said.

Ferelith dragged her fingers across her scalp, rubbing hard, and stared at the ceiling. White. She was heartily sick of the antiseptic white, white, white. Somedays she missed the rainbow-hued fields of hyacinth so much that she physically ached.

The grain fields and orchards on Gefjun were just as colorful — at least, the vids and holos she had seen were colorful. Kilometer after kilometer of amaranth, maize, buckwheat, rye, and fonio, apple and peach and plum and orange and lemon and fig orchards, broken up by wide open fields where tens of thousands of sheep, goats, and cattle roamed free.

She rolled onto her stomach again. "Computer, display filovirus vectors, historical and projected." The screen on the desk above her bed flicked to life, a pulsing red dot positioned right on top of Eidsvoll; smaller green dots marked the hundreds of compounds. The filovirus had originated on one of those compounds, but the animals all mixed together at the main processing center in Eidsvoll; they arrived asymptomatic, but contagious and it had been impossible to trace the virus back to its point of origin. Fifty-two days ago, the first goat to start hemorrhaging had been quarantined, then destroyed. One goat turned into three, into seven, into a dozen. The Ag Compounds locked down their goat populations — and for two days Eidsvoll was virus-free.

Then the cattle began to bleed.

Transport ships from Gefjun were ordered home, or parked in orbit around Hnoss and Gersemi and Iduny and the moons of Frigg while their cargo rotted and panic spread among the people below. Gefjun was the breadbasket of the system; dead, bare rock transformed into an agricultural paradise. Confederacy relief transports would take weeks or months to arrive via the jumpgates, and even then they would bring in enough food for only a fraction of the twenty billion people who called the Helge system home.

Ferelith watched the red circle continue to pulse and expand while the green dots shrank and shrank, turning yellow. The yellow circles pulsed and grew and grew and grew ….

And now the filovirus had broken through *another* species barrier. It was mutating, evolving rapidly, all traces of the original virus — whatever it had been — lost long ago.

She crawled out of bed and knelt before the shrine, feet too sore to hold her upright. She uncorked the vial and the cabin filled with the scent of marglóð, vanilla, honeysuckle, and orange. Flipping the vial, she wet the tip of one finger and gently anointed the statue; the liquid glimmered against the ivory forehead and chest.

She held up her hands. "Golden Apollo, divine healer of all ills, hear my prayer. A sickness has come upon the people and animals of Helge, and your servant has been tasked with protecting and healing them. Cast your golden eyes upon me. Bless my efforts, Apollo, Beautiful God of Plagues."

She fell back into her bed, and slept. She slept, and dreamt of rats and ravens and wolves and blood.

***

Her ear beeped. Ferelith jerked upright, then grunted at the flash of pain in her neck.

Her ear beeped again. She tapped the link. "Henry."

"Apologies, Ferelith. Live com for you from Gefjun."

She swung her legs over the edge of the bed and leaned back, resting her head against the wall. "Patch it through." There was a snap and a loud crackling. "This is Henry."

"Tillie and Kiel are dead."

Ferelith closed her eyes and swallowed hard. "Gods, Sulian, I am so sorry."

"Beaming you the data now."

"Sulian — "

"Three more people at Alpha have fallen ill."

"Sulian — "

"We're on the ground, but there's not much we can do at this point. We brought in two more plasma spinners, but we're just prolonging the inevitable. They're in a lot of pain ...." More loud cracking and a hissing.

Ferelith banged her head against the wall.

"How long?"

She squinted and blinked, focusing on the time stamp in the corner of the computer screen. "Twelve hours. Sulian?"

"... Yes?"

"You left Eidsvoll. You're at Alpha."

" ... I couldn't stay away. There are more vets on this planet than human doctors, and it's my job to take care of these folks."

"I understand." Ferelith exhaled, long and hard, gaze falling on the shrine. The God's forehead and chest were still shiny with perfume. "The pilgrim."

"Pardon?"

"When I was little — seven, actually — my mother and I took the h-train to the Temple of the Olympians in Loen. There was a man in the same car as us, a pilgrim. Adelian leprosy. Not contagious, but … well, he was ugly and he stank and he was in a great deal of pain and the way the other passengers looked at him or refused to look at him or ran away…." She drew up her legs, rubbing at her sore feet. "When the h-train arrived, he stood, but dropped his offering. A wreath of laurel leaves and hyacinth, wrapped in blue silk. It was beautiful. I ran over and picked it up to give it back to him — but my mother grabbed me and dragged me away, and I dropped it again. She took me to the bath house and spent an hour scrubbing me down; I didn't understand it then, and I still don't." She drew up her legs and wrapped her arms around her knees. "I never saw that pilgrim again, but I remember the pain and shame and anger in his eyes. I remember that quite clearly."

Silence.

Ferelith frowned. "Sulian?"

" ... Aye, I'm here."

Her computer beeped.

"The data packet's arrived. I'll start looking it over now."

"Feri?"

"Yes?"

"Thank you."

She felt a smile curve across her face. "You are welcome, Suli. We'll see you soon. Henry out."

***

Ferelith raced down the corridor. She squeezed around Mercer, his nose buried in his tablet, and dodged around Gianna and Sage, their steps sluggish with exhaustion. The double doors of the *Ka-la-nu*'s small, raindrop-shaped bridge swished open. Captain Semissee turned at her entrance. They exchanged quick nods, his thick braid slipping off his shoulder, then both turned towards the main screen.

It curved across the front of the room and high overhead, covering nearly one hundred and eighty degrees. Gefjun filled most the screen, spinning slowly. Seventy percent land, there were only rivers and a few massive lakes scattered across its surface. Mountain ranges here and there, with the sharpest peaks concentrated near the northern pole. The rest, fields and meadows and plains, thousands upon thousands of kilometers of open grassland,

and cultivated amaranth, fonio, buckwheat, rye, and maize; even quinoa at some of the higher elevations, and rice along the shores of the lakes. The surface was a patchwork of browns, golds, whites, greens, and purples.

Ferelith stepped further into the bridge as the ship decelerated, sweeping into a high orbit. The plating beneath her sore feet rumbled. She pressed her hand to the bulkhead beside the com station for support; her back and legs were beginning to ache. Too many hours spent hunched over scanners and spinners and tablets.

"Unole, have you updated Sulian as to our arrival?"

The com officer smiled up at her, black hair cut so short that it was a fine fuzz across her skull. "Yes. No new communications from him, though."

The eastern end of Mälaren swung into view, its waters a brilliant blue-grey. Ferelith scowled at the lake, at the planet, willing it to turn faster, the ship to move faster.

The navigator's voice echoed across the room. "Coming up on Eidsvoll Station, Captain. ETA … four minutes."

"Thank you, Mr. Akae. Dr. Henry?" Semissee pulled his braid over his shoulder, the blue and white ribbons woven through it flashing in the low light, and casually clasped his hands behind his back.

She tilted her chin at the planet below them. "I needed to see it."

Another short nod.

The far shore of Mälaren rotated towards them.

"Eidsvoll Elevator coming into view, Captain."

Ferelith sucked in a breath. Beside her, Unole let out a low grunt. Semissee just frowned.

Ships. Ships upon ships upon ships, transports of every shape and size and age, crowded around the silent elevator. Its base was a gray and green smear: Eidsvoll proper, a rough circle along the western banks of Mälaren. The elevator rose up through the clouds, half a kilometer wide, studded with antennae and lights. Up, and up, and up, a full five hundred kilometers. At the far end, Eidsvoll Station anchored the elevator, a flower of docks stacked and staggered one atop another.

Silent. Still. Locked down.

"Gods help us," Ferelith murmured.

Unole lifted one hand to the mic in her ear, pressing it closer. "Greetings from Eidsvoll Station, Captain. They are granting us emergency permission to descend. And ...," she almost rolled her eyes, " ... they are reminding us to observe all isolation and quarantine measures."

Ferelith *did* roll her eyes.

The Captain's hands tightened, just a bit. "Thank you, Ms. Tikahche. Please alert the crew. If you would, Mr. Akae."

Overlapping "aye, sirs." Ferelith lowered herself into a chair beside Unole, pulling the criss-crossing straps over her chest and waist. Unole followed suit, her voice tingling in Ferelith's ear as she warned the crew to prepare for atmospheric entry. Semissee stayed on his feet, legs braced; he never sat down; not once in the eight years since he had taken command of the *Ka-la-nu* had she seen him sit during entry.

Mr. Akae's fingers tak-tak-taked at the controls, and the elevator slipped away. Gefjun filled the entire screen. The *Ka-la-nu*'s nose tipped up. Her belly hit atmosphere. The bulkhead shook. The screen turned to streaks of red and orange and brilliant white. Ferelith cinched her straps tighter and reminded herself to breathe.

The rumbling gradually lessened. The screen cleared, the fiery light giving way to the arc of the northern shore of Mälaren and the blue squiggle that was the Stig River; the river's warmer waters were a pale fan against Mälaren's cool, deep, blue-grey.

"Mesosphere achieved. ETA Agricultural Compound Alpha … seventy-two minutes."

"Thank you, Mr. Akae. Dr. Henry?"

Ferelith unhooked the straps, wincing as a muscle pulled in her lower back. Hands braced on the chair, she pushed herself to her feet. "We'll be ready."

***

Sulian was waiting for them, body and face hidden by an old-style white biosuit; mud splattered his boots and calves. Slipping her hood over her head, Ferelith caught a glimpse of him on the security screen beside the hatch. He was hunched slightly forward, bracing his legs against the backwash as the thrusters flared. The *Ka-la-nu*'s engines whined, burning irregular circles in the grass. The ship slowed to a hover, rocking a bit as thick landing struts unfolded from its belly. Ferelith grabbed a handhold, steadying herself just as Gianna hit her from behind.

"*Sorry,*" the lab tech mumbled over the com, reaching for her own handhold. She was pale through the clear face mask, with dark smudges around her eyes.

The engines rolled down slowly, the rumble beneath her feet fading.

"Gianna, when was the last time you slept?"

"*Um* ...." The younger woman darted a glance at Tsula and Sage and Mercer and the dozen other doctors, nurses, and techs crammed into the airlock. "*We were all kind of wondering the same thing about you, Dr. Henry.*"

Ferelith tightened her lips. She sealed her face mask into place. "You're right. I haven't been, not well." She twisted around, running her finger along the seam between Gianna's hood and mask; tight and clean. Gianna returned the favor, rising up on her toes. "Bad dreams. *Weird*, bad dreams." She forced herself to smile, first at Gianna, then at everyone else individually. "We all need to follow protocol, me included. Thanks for calling me on it. We'll never beat this bug if we're all too exhausted to think straight."

Tsula pulled on a glove, the tacky lining above the wrist adhering to the sleeve of her biosuit. She squeezed her fingers around it, then held up her arms and let Sage double check the seal. "*Sleep aids?*" she asked.

Ferelith nodded. "As needed. Don't overdo it. Anyone needs to walk away for a minute or an hour to clear your head, do it. Understood?"

Her earlobe tinged. "*Semissee to Response Team. You are cleared for degress.*"

"Copy that." Ferelith checked the rectangular air tank on her thigh, hefted her lab kit, then turned and slapped her hand against the flat red button beside the airlock. It glowed for a moment, vents hissing as internal atmosphere vented back into the ship's cycling system, replaced by planetside air. She knew it was her imagination, but Ferelith could swear she caught a hint of manure, grass, and rain. The button turned green and Ferelith hit it again. The hatch popped and slid gracefully upward, while the ramp extended down. Bright sunlight flooded the airlock.

Ferelith took a step forward, pausing on the threshold to orient herself. The *Ka-la-nu* had set down in a small clearing between the apple orchard and gardens, and the school/recreational center. Her round nose pointed towards the community's hof, and the two dozen godpoles which surrounded it; blue and white wildflowers and bundles of herbs and bowls of honey lay piled around the Eir pole, with smaller offerings to Odin and Thor and Fulla. A rigid, antiseptic, blue-white dome filled the small open space behind the hof. A cluster of yurt-like living quarters stood off to the right, with a few barns and mechanical sheds beyond them. In the distance rose the metal fence, three men high, that kept the free-range herds from trampling the compound; wind turbines and solar panels lined the top. A few automated observation/harvest bots glinted in the sun as they whizzed around in the distance.

Sulian raised a hand. *"Welcome to Gefjun."*

Ferelith returned the gesture, feet slightly unsteady as she descended the ramp. Her boots touched grass and her toes caught. She stumbled, free hand automatically stretching out to latch onto Sulian. He grabbed her elbow. "Sorry. Long night. Thanks for the welcome." She smiled up at him. Warm blue eyes, bracketed by wrinkles of worry and stress, smiled back down at her through the thick helmet. She waved a hand behind her. "You know Tsula. And Gianna, Sage …," and around the group she went, greetings filling her ears.

Sulian nodded at them all, then gestured towards the dome. *"Hospital's this way. We've got six patients now. Agatha is the worst. Frank and Thom aren't doing much better. The other three are in the early stages. The twelve people who are virus-free — so far — are isolated in their homes. Since we still don't know the origins of the virus, we're feeding everyone with d-rations. We're running low."*

"We can get you more." Ferelith moved along beside him. "The bodies?"

Sulian stopped. *" … In the ice house, behind the barns. Triple sealed inside coffin bags."*

Ferelith pushed aside the image of a too-small body inside one of those black bags. She nodded briskly, and waved Gianna and a few of the other techs towards the ice house. A second group broke off and headed towards the living quarters, leaving only her, Sulian, Tsula, and Mercer. She wrapped her free hand around Sulian's elbow, gently tugging him towards the hospital dome. "Come and introduce us to our patients."

***

She slept little, despite her stern words to the crew. She took blood samples, saliva samples, stool samples, tear samples. She put human blood under the microscope, cattle blood, goat blood, sheep blood. She tested and retested them, compared them to other samples, older samples, newer samples, samples of dead tissue, samples of live tissue. Soil samples, water samples, plant samples. She ran computer simulations, one after another after another, watching the virus — that awful, insidious, hated virus — grow and change and kill.

Agatha died. Frank died. Thom died. Carole began to bleed.

One by one, they moved the bodies to the ice house.

Ferelith staggered to a halt beside the hof, still feeling the weight of Thom's body on her arms. The cross beams over the door had been bent and carved into the shape of othala, the rune of inheritance, of the ancestors, of protection and home. Scowling, skin itchy with sweat, Ferelith stomped over to the Eir pole. A calm female face smiled back at her, hair long and loose, a mortar and pestle clasped against her chest. "You're not being much help," she snapped at the Goddess.

A gloved hand closed around her shoulder. *"Easy there, Feri."*

"Well, she's not," she muttered.

Sulian led her away, back towards the *Ka-la-nu,* his grasp gentle but firm. *"Time for sleep."*

"No time for sleep," she argued, hating the petulant tone that crept into her voice.

"*Stop being stubborn. Make time.*"

"I need drugs to sleep."

"*Then take some.*" He halted at the foot of the ramp and spun around. He leaned down until his helmet clacked against her face plate. He glared at her, the lines around his eyes deep, and pointed up the ramp. "*Bed, Feri.*" The glare gradually softened. "*Please?*" He raised one hand to touch her faceplate.

She closed her eyes, shoulders drooping. "Very well." Boots scraping, she trudged up the ramp to the airlock.

She wasn't sure, but he might have whispered, "*Pleasant dreams.*"

***

She was in her mother's perfume studio: the wooden table, the mortar and pestle, knives and spoons, the jars of herbs and flowers, phials of essential oils, bundles of freshly harvested hyacinth laid out or hung from the low beams. Warm morning sunlight spilled in through the windows and the open top half of the door. Outside, she could see her mother's garden: hyacinth in a dozen different colors, interspersed with rosemary and mint and bee balm, native purple-blue phylly and orange cashala and towering purple-black sunseekers.

She was naked, the floorboards smooth beneath her feet.

A woman pushed open the lower door, basket filled with flowers slung over one arm, a wide-brimmed hat on her head. The knees of her canvas trousers were stained, and her fingernails were dark with dirt. Her sun-streaked brown hair was pulled into a loose braid and freckles dotted her nose and cheeks.

Her mother.

But not.

The woman's mouth pulled into an exasperated moue. "Stubborn child." The woman paced over to the table and plopped down the basket; she began to pull out the flowers, arranging them in neat piles. "I admire your determination, but not when it skews into a self-defeating stubbornness. He's been fairly screaming at you, but you've been too exhausted to notice or understand." She shook her head and pulled the mortar and pestle closer. "If you are going to chide the Gods, be sure you have good cause for doing so. In this case, you most certainly did not." She lifted bundles of rosemary from the beam over her head. "This time, pay attention."

There was a low, musical whistle from the door. A bright blue bird, black head crest and striped white tail flaring, settled on the ledge.

The woman turned and smiled. Her voice softened in welcome and affection. "Ah, my little bluebird." She turned back to Ferelith and motioned with her head. "He will show you the way. Pay attention."

Ferelith found herself walking forward. She lifted the latch and pushed the door open, the wood worn down in that one spot by decades of use. The blue bird hopped up onto her left shoulder, trilling softly, tiny claws digging into her skin. Through the garden, the gravel digging into the soles of her feet; sunseekers leaned towards her, over the path, their velvety heads brushing her cheeks and hair. The bird danced on her shoulder, one wing sliding softly across her neck. Out the back gate, which should have opened onto a community greenspace lined with more houses; instead, it was a field of amaranth, the tall beaded heads shading from magenta to deep purple.

The blue bird chirped and leapt off into the sky. Ferelith called after him, or thought she did. She was running, running, chasing him through the field. Sharp leaves cut her arms and legs. She squinted her eyes against the bright sky, straining to keep him in sight. Running, running. She stumbled, caught herself, and was running again.

The field of amaranth and the sky of blue ended, giving way to bare rock and black starry sky. She slid to an abrupt, confused halt.

A wolf stood before her. Huge, black, with golden eyes, he sat on his haunches, tail curled around his paws. The blue bird swooped low and settled once more on her shoulder. The wolf regarded her silently.

"I'm sorry," she thought she heard herself saying. "I've been told that I haven't been paying attention. And, I haven't. I am now. Please, show me again."

The wolf blinked slowly, and then he was gone, running across the rock. Ferelith followed, legs pumping. Pebbles cut into her feet. Fast, so fast. She strained, chest burning, gasping.

A crevice loomed ahead of them, the rock streaked grey and brown. The wolf leapt. Fur dropped away, feathers erupted, and the wolf became a raven. Flapping, he sped over the gorge, a shiny black streak against the star-filled sky. Sobbing, chest hot and tight, the blue bird shrieking in her ear, Ferelith threw herself forward, up, forward, over.

She fell and slid and rolled, skin and muscles scrapping against rock. Hissing, bruised and bleeding, she picked herself up. She looked around wildly, hunting the sky. The blue bird jumped off her shoulder, winging away. Limping, pushing herself faster, Ferelith chased after him, his striped blue and white tail bright in the night.

There. There he was. The raven, his feathers gleaming. The blue bird returned, clinging tight.

She followed the raven, arms pumping hard, her knees shaking as she strained to climb a steep hill. She grabbed at the rock to pull herself up. It hurt. She kept climbing. She stopped at the summit, head tilted back. The sky spread out above her; Hnoss and Gersemi were twin points of greenish-blue light, Iduny more distant and more brown; Frigg was a dull reddish-yellow, her moons invisible to the naked eye.

The raven circled, loosing a harsh caw, then dove down the far side of the hill.

Ferelith followed, stumbling and tumbling. She fell, banging her knees hard, pulled herself back up again.

The raven veered towards the ground. Feathers blew away and fur sprouted. An enormous rat dropped to the hard rock, tail as long as his body. Bright yellow eyes peered at her, his nose twitching. And then he was gone, scuttling away, disappeared.

"Wait," Ferelith thought she croaked, throat dry, chest too tight.

Again, the blue bird hopped off her shoulder. Gliding forward, he circled, then settled on a large, vaguely pyramidal boulder. He pranced, the black crest of feathers on his head fanning wide.

Ferelith limped over to the boulder.

A hole. There was a hole in the ground, half hidden by the boulder.

She could hear the rat, its squeaks echoing.

Gingerly, she lowered herself to the ground, the rock cold against her bare skin. A pebble dug into her breast. She squeezed her head into the hole, then her arms and shoulders. The blue bird chirped and landed on her back. He danced, claws poking her. She wiggled further into the hole, following the squeaks. She dug her fingers into the loose rock and soil, pulling herself forward; she pushed with her toes; harder. Grunting, clawing, she wrestled her way through the narrow tunnel.

Her hands touched air, cool and damp. The lip of the tunnel gave way and she slid forward and down, down, down. With an oof and a painful bang of her elbows, she hit solid ground.

Panting, she pushed herself upright.

Dark. It was completely dark. She could hear the rat, squeaking and chittering, feet pattering across the stone. And water. A steady trickle into a larger body of water. Feathers touched her cheek and the blue bird settled on her shoulder again.

"I can't see," she thought she said.

And then she could. It was still dark, but she could see clearly.

The cave was small, barely large enough to hold three people. Water dribbled down the opposite wall, a dull red stain spreading across the rock. A shallow pool covered most of the cave's floor, an ugly, angry red. In the center of the pool stood the rat, eyes bright gold. His mouth opened wide. Teeth sharp, he raced across the top of the water and launched himself at Ferelith.

She screamed —

***

She bolted upright in her bed, clothes sticky with sweat. The lights automatically flicked on. Panting, blinking rapidly, she looked around her quarters, momentarily confused.

Her eyes settled on the shrine. The faintest trace of marglóð still shone on the idol's chest and forehead.

Ferelith swung her legs over the side of the bed, and immediately stopped. She groaned. Her whole body hurt. She stretched tentatively and wobbled to her feet. Pulling the stopper off the phial of marglóð, she tipped it to moisten her finger and anointed the statue again: forehead, chest, belly, hands, and feet. She set down the phial and lifted her palms.

"Beautiful God, bright Apollo, Lord of the wolf, the raven, and the rat: my gratitude, forever and always."

Wincing, she hurried as fast as she could out the door and towards the airlock. She tapped her earlobe. "Henry to Sulian."

"*Feri? You sound awful —*"

"I need maps. Maps of Gefjun, before and after it was terraformed. And a rover. Your best rover. We're taking a trip."

***

Amaranth heads smacked against the roll bars of the vehicle, spraying seeds; they filled her lap, bounced off her face mask. She brushed a few off the tablet, clutching it tight against her chest. She expanded the image, tabbing back and forth between the two topographical maps.

"Keep going! Due north!"

An automated observation/harvest bot paralleled their course for a few moments, hovering in seeming confusion. It beeped and flashed, then zipped away.

Hands tight on the wheel, Sulian shot her a quick glance. In his bulky old biosuit, he barely fit in the seat. *"I keep telling you, there's nothing out this way. It's scrubland. Too rocky for crops. Even the goats don't like it out here."*

"Exactly."

"What?"

She shook her head. The amaranth field thinned and then abruptly ended, giving way to sparse grass, shrubs, and rock. "We should be coming up on the gorge. How do we get across?"

"We go ten kilometers east or about fifteen kilometers west."

"Those are the closest bridges?" She zoomed in the map.

"*There **aren't** any bridges. Never bothered to build any because no one ever comes out here.*"

Ferelith shook her head again. She could see the gorge. It hadn't been this big in her dream …. Carole was bleeding. Tobias was bleeding. Sven had moved into the hospital dome, his body hot and aching. "We don't have time for a detour."

Sulian muttered something about Hel's tits and slammed his foot down on the accelerator. The rover shot forward, pushing Ferelith back in her seat. They raced towards the gorge, tires spitting rock. Ferelith grabbed the roll bar with one hand. She might have screamed. Or maybe it was Sulian.

The rover hit the edge of the crevice, arced up. Ferelith saw sky. The tires continued to spin. Down, down, the ground rising up, up, up, faster. The rover slammed into the hard stone, bounced, slammed again. Her air tank and portable lab kit dug into her thigh. She lost the tablet; it clattered down by her feet. The rover swerved, shot forward again.

Sulian grinned at her, eyes shining. "*How's that for a first date?*"

She laughed, a giddy, hysterical edge to the sound. She strained against the safety straps and pulled the tablet back into her lap. "West, just a bit." She waved her hand. "Towards that hill."

" ... *That's not a hill, Feri. That's practically a mountain.*"

"Then we're going up the mountain."

The scrubland gave way to pure rock, only a few hardy bushes poking out of cracks here and there. The ground angled up gradually, then more sharply.

"*How far?*"

"Down the other side. Look for ... look for a bunch of boulders."

Sulian cranked the wheel, finding a slightly level path.

"Where are you going?"

"*Faster this way. Around, instead of up and over.*"

The engine whined. Tires slid, gripped, slid again.

"*Tell me again why we couldn't take the shuttle?*" he demanded, shifting gears.

"I needed to see it. The ground. I needed to see the path."

He might have grunted.

The ground leveled out again, then angled, then tipped as Sulian spun the wheel around and headed straight down the far side of the mountain. The rover bounced and pitched. She lost the tablet again, and clung to the roll bar with both hands. The safety straps bit into her shoulders. The rear end of the rover tipped up dangerously, then slammed back down, rattling her teeth.

175

"*Is that it?*"

"What? Where?"

"*Over there!*" He jerked an elbow, hands clenched tight around the wheel.

Ferelith peered off to her right. A jumble of boulders and smaller rocks, one oddly pyramidal … "I think — yes! Yes, that's it!" She pointed frantically. "Over there!"

The rover veered towards the boulders. Pebbles flew and brakes squealed as Sulian pulled the vehicle to a hard stop. Hands shaking, Ferelith unbuckled the safety straps, awkwardly shoving them back off her shoulders. She clambered out, her air tank and kit banging, searching for the pyramid-shaped boulder. Sulian took even longer to get out of the rover, banging his helmet against the roll bar twice. He heaved himself out, grunting.

"It was right here — yes, over there!" She dashed forward. As with the gorge and the mountain, the pyramidal rock was much bigger in reality than it had been in her dream — and so was the hole. She crouched at the edge, cautious of the crumbling rim. Loose soil dribbled into the gaping crack. She peered over, tapping the button on the side of her face mask. Tiny lights embedded in the outer seam of the mask flashed to life, illuminating the first few meters of the tunnel. She would have to crouch, but at least she wouldn't have to crawl. She shivered, remembering the dark, narrow tunnel of the God-sent dream.

176

"Hold on." Sulian threw a harness over her head and around her waist. She twisted around, and saw that one end was attached to the rover. He tightened the harness. *"Watch your step. I'm too big to come after you if there's a problem."*

She nodded, and stepped into the tunnel. It was level for about half a meter, then dropped almost vertical. She slipped, clutching the harness, and stumbled the rest of the way into the cave.

There was just enough light from her face mask to illuminate the cavern. It was just like the dream the God had gifted her: the trail of water along the far wall, the smear of dull red, and the wide shallow pool. The water was thick, a congealed, bloody red.

"Feri?"

"Yes, it's here. It's here. Hold on." Her fingers fumbled. She pulled the lab kit off her thigh and knelt at the edge of the pool. She flipped open the case, found the test strip and phial of suspension fluid she needed, and gently scooped a sample of the water. *Apollo, smile on me.* She shook the phial, the red water mixing with the suspension fluid. The strip turned black.

She screamed. "Yes, this is it! Sulian, this is it! The original virus, we found it! We found it!"

***

Spinners whirled, tubes bubbled. Two different iterations of the filovirus rotated slowly above the table: the ancient, indigenous virus, born on a rocky, untouched world; and the mutated filovirus, transformed even as Gefjun was reborn, which killed men and women and children and cattle. One simulation after another charted the mutation of the virus, the holomatrix shivering.

Carole died. Tobias died. Sven began to bleed. Katherynne began to bleed.

The first simulated vaccine failed. The second failed. The third stopped the new filovirus. They brewed up batch. Ferelith tapped the side of the plexisteel habitat. One of the mice lifted his head and looked directly at her, nose twitching. She reached in and lifted him out. Murmuring a thanks, stroking his head, she held him still while Tsula injected him with first the vaccine, then the virus.

The mouse died.

Sven died.

They brewed up a fourth batch. Ferelith tapped the side of the habitat, thanked the mouse who responded, and held him close while he was injected.

Katherynne died.

The mouse lived.

They injected three more mice. They all lived.

"My turn." Ferelith rolled up her sleeve. Tsula raised her eyebrows, and silence settled around the lab. "Human trials are the next logical step. If it works, we can begin planet-wide inoculations." She waved her bare arm. Tsula scowled. "I'm not carrying anyone else into that damned ice house."

Tsula exhaled long and hard. She swabbed Ferelith's arm. "You better not die. I'm most senior after you, and I really do *not* want your job."

Gianna snorted.

The first hypo stung, then the second. They slapped remote monitoring disks on the side of her head, on her chest, her belly, the back of one hand. And they waited. One hour, two, three. Heart rate, respiration, blood pressure, all remained normal. Tsula drew a blood sample and threw it under a microscope; the holomatrix flashed, the two viruses disappearing to be replaced by a handful of her cells.

Healthy cells.

Dead viruses, shriveled and stained bluish-black, floated in their wake.

Gianna squealed. Mercer whooped, spinning in a wild circle. Ferelith collapsed into a chair, burying her face in her hands.

Thank you, Apollo. Thank you, Eir. Thank you.

***

The formula for the vaccine was beamed to the only hospital in Eisdvoll, to Eidsvoll Station, to the Med Temple on Iduny, and to every other medical complex in the system. They spun up a large enough batch in the lab on the *Ka-la-nu* to vaccinate the crew, Sulian, and the surviving fifteen members of Ag Compound Alpha.

The funerals came next: Tillie and Kiel and Agatha and Frank and Thom and Carole and Tobias and Sven and Katherynne. Their bodies were flash burned in the ship's medical incinerator, reduced to less then ash and compressed into tiny, glossy black cubes. The cubes were carefully placed in a wooden box covered in othala and fehu and gebo and wunjo runes, and buried in the ancestral plot behind the school.

Next came the offerings. They gathered inside the hof, its walls lined with altars for the Gods and Goddesses and ancestors. Thanks were given to Eir and Odin and Fulla and Thor, with a special plea to Hel to welcome their loved ones to her banquet. A small table was brought in, with a candle and bowl of honey for Apollo; Ferelith lit the candle and set the crow feather from Delphi beside it.

And then they celebrated. Apple cider and honey mead, roast lamb and beef, spinach and raspberries and kale and pecans and herb goat cheese. A bonfire was set, turning the *Ka-la-nu*'s opalescent hull to glittering orange-gold. Drums were brought forth, and horns and a violin and Mercer even dug out his flute. Unole spun Sage around the fire while Mr. Akae regaled a gaggle of children with stories of his years flying for the Confederacy, and Tsula pulled Captain Semissee down onto a log to rebraid her lover's hair; she used pink ribbons, this time.

From the far side of the fire, Sulian saluted Ferelith with a glass of apple cider. He grinned when she returned the salute and wandered over.

"So that's what you look like outside an antiquated biosuit." She tilted her head back to look up at him. He was a full head taller than her, with the broad shoulders and firm hips of a farmer. His hair was black and curly (not too long), and his eyes an even brighter blue now that they weren't obscured by a helmet. Practical canvas pants and thick-soled boots and a dark red shirt buttoned at the wrists.

He grinned again. "And that's what you look like outside a fancy, top of the line biosuit."

"We've got extra. We can leave you a few before we take off."

His grin wavered and he took a long drink from his glass. "And when will that be?"

She shrugged, watching Sage and Unole spin in a slow, seductive circle around Mercer. "A week or so. We need to make sure the inoculations take. And the animal vaccines are still only in the simulation stage. We need to get those field tested …. It's pretty here," she blurted.

"Aye," Sulian agreed slowly. "Part of the reason I settled on Gefjun. I liked the look of the place. The smell, too: rain and grass and apples. Got a couple in my yard."

"Apple trees?"

He nodded, gaze settling on her. "Apricot and plum trees, too."

" …. Sounds nice," she said, following him as he lowered himself to an empty log. They sat silently for long moments, watching the fire and the dancers and the drummers. Sage and Unole disappeared into the orchard, Mercer following, still playing his flute. "I was thinking," she began, hesitating.

"Mm?" He set down his empty glass and began rolling up his sleeves.

"Working on the *Ka-la-nu* … it's not as satisfying as it used to be. I think I need a change of scenery. I was wondering — " She stumbled to a halt, eyes fixed on Sulian's left forearm. "That's — um," she swallowed " — that's a nice tattoo."

"What, this?" He lifted his arm, the firelight illuminating the deep black and blue and white. "Adelian bluebird. That's where I got my start. Interned at a temple there during the last leprosy outbreak. There were colonies of them nesting in the apple trees outside the temple proper. Their song … well, it was the only thing that could comfort the patients. And the doctors." He shook his head. "All that technology, all those brilliant medical minds, and all we could do was pray and listen to the birds sing."

Ferelith set aside her glass and slid her hand down his arm, across the tattoo, linking her fingers through his; they fit together well. "I hear there are plenty of veterinarians on Gefjun, but not enough human doctors. Think you could use one more?"

Sulian tightened his fingers around hers, and smiled.

Daphne's Errand

by Maggie Koger

Day One

I've been out of society for some time now and I usually don't answer the door unless I'm expecting a delivery or the help, but it was a bright morning and I had gotten up quite early to dig a flower bed at the back of the house where I planned to plant some flower bulbs for next spring. So I had just come in when the knocker sounded, and before I knew it a young woman was standing in front of me holding a dress bag on a hanger and carrying a shoebox.

"Good morning," I said, trying to be as polite as I could.

"I have the dress and shoes your wife wanted — a Mrs. James Alstead," the woman answered.

"Well, I am James Alstead and there must be some error," I said. "My wife did not order any clothing."

"Not that she ordered, sir. It's that she *wanted.*"

I didn't care much for such a smart answer from someone half my age because my wife kept to her room those days, she only wore a dress and shoes on her birthday when I told her that her father was coming. I'd pretend he'd been delayed and after she'd had her cake and tea she would go back to her room and lie down — I would tell her that he'd be along later. She'd sleep, and after sundown I'd change her into nightclothes. I used to give her a birthday every week but it got to be too much trouble.

"My wife doesn't want whatever you've got there," I told the woman at the door. "She can't have what she wants and she has given up on everything else, so please leave us in peace." I started to close the door when I heard Laurel's voice calling from the bedroom.

"Has father come?" she asked — her voice whiny with longing.

"No, Laurel, it's not your birthday today." I was afraid she would start one of her crying spells, so I added, "It's tomorrow, dear."

I hated the weeping days. Sometimes if I read poetry to her she would come out of it; other times I would give up and play the radio so I couldn't hear her. After the twins and her father died, she never recovered. I was gone when the twins died and her father brought them here to be buried at his old place in the country. Laurel never left. It's very isolated, and when he died there was no one to keep her company. Some folks did come, but Laurel talked about nothing but the boys and her father — how they were all working or playing in the orchard, or gone down to the barn, or out hunting quail, or fishing. Everyone knew they were up at the cemetery and so the townspeople just quit trying. The place was a mess when I finally arrived, so I resigned my commission and scoured the countryside for help. After a number of tries, I found a widow woman who came faithfully once a week. That's been years ago now.

When I looked out of the door again I saw that the woman holding the dry goods was extraordinarily beautiful and she that looked a good deal like my wife had before the war.

"You must look at the dress, Mr. Alstead." With that the woman pushed into the room, stood beside me and unzipped the dress bag. Forgive me, but I hardly saw what she was holding at the moment because I could not stop looking at her. I noticed the large wooden bracelets on her wrists, wide bands carved in twining stems and sequenced leaves. And she wore a long patterned dress, very unusual for a delivery job, and it too had a series of branches with leaves almost sculpted into the fabric. As I looked, the leaves seemed to rustle about in the sunlight — I had never seen anything quite like it. And when I looked straight into her eyes they were bright blue, and then I saw how her golden hair flowed across her shoulders in waves. She pressed the dress hanger into my hands, dropped the shoebox on the floor and swept past me to the door.

"It's what she wants, Mr. Alstead, she must wear it seven days and you must wash it each night that she does in cool water. It will be dry in the mornings, and you will know when it is time for her to wear it again. I'll return to check on her soon."

The dress was white and gauzy with lace and such. The hanger must have weighed more than the dress, and although the woman had been strange enough, I thought I would play along. I kicked the unopened shoe box into the coat closet and went into the bedroom. "Laurel dear," I said, "It's your birthday after all." And later after I had gathered up her lunch tray — she hardly ate anything these days — I slipped her nightgown off and slid the dress over her head. I gave her a mirror so she could see the lacy collar softening her thin face as I buttoned about a thousand tiny white buttons. The dress had a long, full skirt and puffy sleeves. I didn't think of it then, but it looked something like the christening gowns we used for the boys. The gowns were heirlooms — even her father and his twin had worn them. For all of that, the dress could have been a wedding dress — you know the type. It took a long time to dress her, but when she was ready I defrosted a couple of cupcakes and we had tea. As we ate, it seemed to me that the late afternoon light had dimmed to a shadow, and when I looked at my wife her cheeks were smooth and glowing. I felt like the leaf lady had brought us some kind of relief. I wondered who she was and when she would return.

That night I washed the dress in cool water and hung it up to dry like I was supposed to.

Day Seven

It seemed like a year went by after the "seven days" began, but in reality only a week had passed. The dress must have been developed using some new technology, because it changed after each washing. Initially the fabric thickened and the lace seemed to melt away. Seams in the bodice multiplied into an unevenly smocked pattern somewhat like tree branches appear when viewed from the ground. Beads shaped like blossoms flowered on the collar and cuffs as the sleeves lengthened. Later the collar disappeared entirely and the neckline widened, first to a sweetheart shape, and then it deepened into an attractive V, revealing a goodly portion of my wife's décolletage. The color shifted as well, first a lightly mottled sandy tone and then a creamy vanilla emerged. My wife grew more active, washing herself and helping me dress her. Sometimes she even touched up her lips and cheeks to a blush color. I thought of John Lyle's poem about the nymph, "On Daphne's Cheeke grow Rose and Cherry, / On Daphne's Lip a sweeter Berry." Her hair softened and began to shine again when the sun was full out. I had no way of accounting for these changes, but all in all she looked a good deal younger. We had six "birthdays," the dress growing more fetching and shimmery for each one. Later that day would have been the seventh celebration, but then the knocker on the door sounded. I hated to answer, but I did.

With fall setting in, most of the leaves had fallen from the trees east of the drive, so the morning sun had sharpened. When I opened the door, my eyes were struck with light so brilliant it blackened what I could see of the outer shape of our visitor. High to his right, he held up an old-fashioned musical instrument, something like a small harp. I forgot my manners and called immediately to Laurel, "It's Lord Byron and he's brought Apollo's lyre to play for your birthday!" I was thinking of the lines, "I wish to tune my quivering lyre, / To deeds of fame, and notes of fire." I started to repeat them for her, when the man stepped forward. He began to strum the harp with a small pick and as soon as the music reached my ears I felt curiously acquiescent, ushering him quickly into the house and calling Laurel again. When she came from the bedroom, I saw that her dress had returned to its frothy white appearance. He beckoned for us to follow him and we did, as if he were a piper who had rights to our very beings. We plunged into the woods and were soon sitting beside a small stream. I don't know how long we were there, but it seemed as if I awoke much later and realized that the music had stopped. When we looked around, the man was gone and I wondered then what he had wanted. I'm glad now that I didn't know. Laurel and I felt totally elated by the musical interlude, and when we returned to the house we spent the last few hours of the day absorbed in a renewed interest in each other — so there was no time for cake and tea. I barely remembered to wash the dress that evening. I've often wondered if I used too much soap, or if the water was too hot. The next morning the dress had streaks of brown and green as if it had meadow soil rubbed in. Laurel cried out at the sight of it, ran back into the bedroom and stayed there.

I hung the dress outdoors on the clothesline hoping the sun would restore the fabric. I knew I couldn't wash it until evening, so I busied myself to finish the bulb planting. I dug the ground in a half circle at the foot of the laurel tree. You may be more familiar with the term "bay," as we call the leaves dried for use as a spice. I thought the showy accents of tulips would adorn the trunk of the evergreen with a hopeful promise-of-summer look next spring, something like a colorful necklace. I thought sadly of how Laurel had seemed to come around with the dress and all, but I couldn't imagine what would happen next — if she would recover, if the dress would. Then I saw the woman standing beside the tree. She was the same woman who had brought the dress, but she seemed older, and her hair was a dull blonde shade. Her clothes were darker—grungy field boots, brown pants and a limp green blouse. I gestured toward the dress.

"I'll need to wash it in the stream," was all she said. She took hold of the dress and walked to the woods. She seemed to grow taller and indistinct in the distance and I saw her looking back once, but she didn't speak.

Day Eight

The next morning I found the dress hanging from the bay tree. It was greatly changed, a brown homespun fabric with embroidered wreaths of leaves around the neck and sleeves. I was afraid Laurel would never wear it, but she didn't seem to notice the transformation. I asked her if today was her birthday and she just looked at me, so I went out back and started to burn some dry leaves.

Day Thirty-Nine

A month has passed without incident and Laurel hasn't spoken much at all, but at least there doesn't seem to be a pall of sorrow hanging over her. She wears the dress from morning until night, spending her days sitting in the rocker on the front porch and knitting a white afghan. I asked her who it was for and she said, "He'll come again and I'll be ready this time."

When I remembered the shoebox and opened it — it was empty.

The Oracle of Delphi

by Joe Giordano

Jenna and Stacie walked along a bubbling stream and approached a blue pool of water nestled in the rocks east of the Delphi temple.

Jenna said, "Oh my God. It's the Kassotis Spring. I'm going in."

The bright orange glow of sunrise spilled over the rocky crests of Mount Parnassus. A shroud of morning fog plunged down to a green gorge, then swept upwards to rocky brown hills in distant focus. The cool air carried the sound of calling birds and water gurgling over rocks. A handful of Doric columns stuck skyward like mangled fingers and glinted pink and gray in the early sunlight. Jenna was blonde with gray eyes. Stacie was a redhead with a pug nose.

Stacie grabbed her head. "What are you doing? You're insane."

Jenna threw panties onto her pile of clothes. She put a foot into the water. "Damn, it's cold."

"Not so loud."

Jenna sank into the current, and the water enveloped her. "It's not bad once you're in." Jenna lay back and floated. She took long breaths. Her blonde hair spread on the water like a lily pad.

Stacie broke the trance. "Jenna, let's not get arrested on our vacation."

Jenna emerged slowly, her body flushed and dripping. Stacie threw her the towel they'd brought from the hotel.

Jenna patted herself. "I went instantly into meditation. For hundreds of years oracles purified themselves in preparation for Apollo's divine inspiration."

"I'm sure it was orgasmic. Thank God no one saw you. I can hear the newscast, 'Cops picked up a modern day Dionysian Maenad this morning. The woman was naked and suspected drunk.' By the way, I suggest some all-body tanning work. Your shiny white ass nearly blinded me."

Jenna smirked.

Jenna and Stacie picked their way along the jagged rocks and scrubby brush to the temple. A large black altar stood at the foot of the temple's east entrance.

Jenna put her arm around her friend. "The priest brings a supplicant to where we are now. A tethered goat bleats. The priest grabs the animal's horns and slits its throat. At the far end of the cella, a huge ivory and gold cult statue of Apollo looms, dimly lit by oil lamps. A floating mist rises through an opening in the marble floor. Below, the oracle in gilt-edged white sits on a bronze tripod that straddles the fissure source of the vapor."

Stacie smiled. "Then, a voice rings out, 'Zeus the all-seeing grants to Athenian prayer that the wooden walls, only, shall not fall but help you and your children.' Themistocles builds spear ships, there's the Battle of Salamis, and Xerxes goes home with his tail between his legs."

Jenna eyed the red-letter sign in both English and Greek that prohibited entrance into the temple ruins.

Stacie raised her palms. "Jenna, no."

"Hell yes." Jenna scampered past the rope barrier, up the stone ramp, and onto the temple remains.

"Jenna, the Greeks take their antiquities seriously. This isn't amusing."

"Either come on or shush." Jenna's head shifted quickly, and her eyes lighted on a gap in the block floor. She disappeared into the hole like a rabbit.

Stacie said, "Oh my God." She turned and looked around. The site was still empty.

The *adyton* had no steps. Jenna dropped down into a gap in the earth. The space was pitch dark with a silence felt in the teeth. She plopped down onto a cool rock. Her heart pounded. A musky sweet scent rose from the earth. Jenna's breaths were measured. On exhales her body felt heavy. Her mind hummed like a Tibetan incantation, and she heard the flap of birds' wings high overhead.

She was shaken by a shout.

"Jenna, what the hell are you doing? I can't see you. Are you all right?"

"Go away."

"Have you lost your mind?"

"I like it here."

194

"Please come out. You're scaring me."

"Damn." Jenna shook her head. "Okay. Help me up."

Stacie reached down and yanked Jenna into the daylight. She didn't let go of Jenna's hand until they were off the prohibited area.

"Stop pulling. Now I know how a newborn feels when it's yanked out of its mother."

"The baby didn't volunteer to go into the womb. Do you intend to act this nuts for the entire trip?"

"I was in the holy of holies. It was transcendental."

"Does the term 'narcissistic' mean anything to you? You go down a wormhole and come out the Maharishi Yogi? Give me a break. Let's get back to Athens."

As they walked toward the exit, Jenna said, "I'm not taking the bus."

"What does that mean?"

"I have a bad feeling. No bus."

"Is this the enlightenment you received in your cavelet?"

"You can ridicule if you like. No bus."

"How do we get back?"

"We hitchhike."

"In a foreign country? Do you think all the crazies live in the States?"

"If the driver gives me the creeps, we won't get in."

"Brilliant."

195

A driver stopped who spoke English. He had a large black mustache. A red, Communist Party hammer and sickle emblem was stuck on his back window.

"You go to Athens?"

Stacie said, "Great guess. Were you down the rabbit hole with my friend Alice?"

"What?"

"Never mind. What's your name?"

"Giorgos. *Hero polli.*"

"I'm Stacie, that's Jenna. Thanks for the ride." They both got in.

Giorgos was in his thirties and worked at Coca-Cola *Tria Epsilon*.

He said, "*Eufaristo* for visiting Greece. So many tourists are afraid to come."

Stacie in the back said, "We hear snippets in the States about the economic crisis. What's the real story?"

Giorgos shook his head. "Capitalists squeeze their workers like lemons and shield their obscene profits from tax. The old have their pensions cut; young people see no future. Europe and our politicians throw ashes in our eyes. I don't know what will become of us."

Jenna's face began to glow. She raised her hands. "The tears of the people rise to the firmament. Apollo Delphinus will bless a new hero. Ambrosia and nectar will flow again in the land of Hellas."

Giorgos did a double take at her.

Stacie sighed. "Jenna, what was that?"

Jenna slumped. "Exhausting."

Stacie said, "Was that some sort of prophecy?"

"If it walks like a prophecy, and quacks . . . Well, you know."

"When self-absorption leads to fantasy, it's time to see a doctor."

Giorgos said to Jenna, "You're not well?"

Jenna glared at Stacie. "I'm fine."

Giorgos dropped the girls at the hotel. He refused gas money. "You're guests in my country. Hospitality is very important in Greece."

The Hotel Panorama was in the Plaka, the old part of the city. The girls looked up to see the Acropolis; its gray-white marble sparkled against an intense blue sky.

The owner of the hotel, Mr. Papanikolaou, rushed to them. He had a military bearing and a deep scar from ear to chin.

"Ladies, I'm so glad you're okay. Have you heard? A tour bus from Delphi had a terrible accident on the National Road. It's on the news."

Stacie said, "That's horrible."

"Yes, it's a *tragodia*. Many were injured. Someone gave you a ride. That's good fortune."

Stacie said, "Is the Red Cross collecting money for victims? We'd like to help."

Mr. Papanikolaou smiled. It softened his scar. "That's so kind. I'll find out." He walked into the hotel.

Jenna tilted her head at Stacie.

Stacie raised her hand. "Don't say it."

"I'm not gloating. People have been hurt."

"It's well known psychology that when something occurs that we've forecasted, we remember but forget all the times our predictions were wrong."

"Apollo gave Cassandra the gift of prophecy, but no one believed her."

"Oh, please."

Jenna stopped short. Her face clouded.

Stacie said, "What?"

"Your mother will call."

Stacie's cell phone played her mother's ring tone.

Stacie's brow furrowed. She hit "speaker" on the phone.

Her mother's voice was tense. "Stacie, there's nothing to worry about, but your father had a little incident."

"Oh my God. What happened?"

Jenna put her hand on her friend's shoulder.

"Honey, he had some chest pain. We brought him to the hospital for tests, and he's had a stent put into one of his arteries. The procedure went well. I didn't want to call until he was able to speak to you. I'll put him on."

Her father's voice was hoarse. "Princess, hi."

"Daddy, are you all right?"

"Just a little tired."

198

"I'll come home on the next plane."

"No, I'm fine. Don't ruin your vacation. You've earned it."

Stacie's eyes were wet. "I want to be with you."

Her father said, "Margaret, speak to her."

Her mother came back on the line. "Stacie, your father's okay. Please don't rush back. We'll call tomorrow. Love you."

"Love you." Stacie hung up. She made a small sob. "He sounded weak."

Jenna hugged her friend's shoulders.

Stacie wiped her eyes. She stiffened and looked at Jenna. "How did you know?"

Jenna shrugged. "I just did."

Stacie stared at Jenna.

Jenna broke the silence. "You look uneasy."

"Don't you think what just occurred was eerie?"

Jenna raised her chin. "I suppose."

"What happened to you in Delphi?"

"It was out-of-body. As if I went back two thousand years."

"Something has changed in you, but I just can't believe . . ." Stacie shook her head. "Never mind."

"Maybe you don't feel like going out tonight?"

"I'd like a little time alone."

"Use the room, I'll go for a run."

Jenna threw on shorts and a tee shirt and headed toward the forest area near the Acropolis. It was warm, there was a scent of pine, and the cicadas were screaming.

A short woman draped in a white, lace veil appeared in Jenna's path.

Jenna jerked back like she'd come to the end of a tether.

The woman raised a bony, alabaster finger pointing at Jenna. Her voice was a growl. "Why stand there doomed one? Fly to the world's end. Apollo rides in a speeding chariot, and will bring you low. Make haste, and bow your heart to grief."

"Who are you? How did you know I speak English?"

The old woman lowered her arm. "I speak in tongues."

"Why is Apollo displeased with me?"

The woman's voice rose. "You've acquired abilities Apollo never intended. This is blasphemy. Relinquish the gift of prophecy before it's too late."

Jenna put a hand to her mouth.

The woman said, "Do it."

Jenna held her head. "I meant no harm. Please."

"Do it before Apollo strikes you with a flaming arrow."

Jenna raised her eyes to heaven. "I foreswear the power." There was a break in the clouds. A ray of sunlight shone through.

A hatless Greek policeman, about twenty-five, with blue eyes, dressed in a dark uniform appeared. He looked at the old woman with hands on hips. "Alka, are you bothering this young lady?"

The old woman turned her head with arm raised as if warding off evil. She stayed silent.

The policeman turned to Jenna. "I'm sorry if Alka was bothering you."

Jenna's face cleared. Her breathing and pulse rate slowed. "It's okay."

Alka moved away.

He said, "Alka is an Albanian immigrant. She makes a few coins offering prophecies to tourists. She's harmless, but we keep watch to see that she doesn't make a pest of herself."

"Prophecies?"

"Yes, Alka is one of the homeless people hospitals had to release because of budget cuts. It's a shame."

"She's mentally disturbed?"

"I'm afraid she's as crazy as an optimistic Athenian."

"How so?"

"She thinks she's the Oracle of Delphi."

Jenna's face reddened. "How could anyone believe that?"

Rites and Recipes

Apollo and the Nine Muses by Gustave Moreau

Anointing Oil Recipe

by Tina Georgitsis

Base Oil: 15 mils Olive Oil
Add: 12 Drops Cinnamon
Add: 1 Dried Laurel Bay Leaf

Instructions: place into a clear dry glass jar in the following order: 1 dried bay laurel leaf, 15 mils of olive oil and 12 drops of cinnamon oil (bark or leaf is fine) and put in the sun for a full day (Sunday is the best day to do this as summertime). After the day is over place out of direct sunlight and succuss (shake the bottle) every day for three weeks and then the oil is ready for use.

New Year's Tribute to Apollo

by Hélio Pires

Since Apollo is a god who stands before the gates, it made sense to me that He should be given a place in what is essentially a chronological doorway, i.e. New Year. This is not an historical association, at least not within Roman polytheism: Janus already fulfilled that role, which probably explains why in Rome Apollo was not associated with gates. As is to be expected with imported deities, the host culture adapts the god to its needs, adding or dropping features as it deems necessary.

But that doesn't mean people shouldn't make the connection today: for one, because the overlapping of divine realms and functions is a natural part of a religious system where the gods are more than just archetypes; and secondly, because there is a difference between learning from the past and being stuck in it.

So in an effort to give Apollo a significant share of my religious life, I devised a small New Year tribute to Him, to take place annually on January 7th. It can stand on its own or be included in a larger ceremony and you are of course free to adapt it to your needs, means and religious tradition.

***

Burn a laurel leaf

I stand at the Gates of Twelve,
past the sun's renewal,
at the start of a new year.
I greet the great son of thundering Zeus,
the shining scion of ancient Leto,
the undying brother of unbound Artemis,
island-born and laurel-crowned god.

Burn a laurel leaf

I praise Apollo,
the bright raven lord,
light-filled cleanser
and remover of death-stain,
destroyer of the old and bringer of the new.
A year has ended, another begins:
thus I honour you with this offering.

Burn incense

I praise Apollo,
the radiant warden,
averter of evil
and lord of boundaries,
the god who stands at the entrance.
I worship you, divine lord,
and welcome you with this offering.

Pour a libation

I praise Apollo,
the luminous lord of health,
father of Asclepius
and divine healer,
the lord of mice and medics.
With clean hands and clear mind,
I give you this offering.

Burn salted flour

I stand before you, Apollo,
at this threshold in time,
with good prayers,
good heart
and in honest tribute.
And I ask you, far-seeing god,
to bless me and my household:

Give us a fresh start, raven lord,
and let misfortune be left behind.
Grant us protection, radiant warden,
and deflect evil from our doorstep.
Keep us healthy, divine healer,
or help us face illness
when we fall prey to it.

Burn a laurel leaf

At the start of a new year,
I welcome you, Apollo.
On this seventh day of January,

I honour you, bright lord.
And with this final offering to you,
Apollo, lyre-playing god,
know that my devotion is sincere.

Pour a libation

Offering to Apollo

by Callum Hurley

My Lord Apollo,
Pheobus, Delius;
I pray that you accept this — my devotion
From my soul unto page
Votive to thine eye —
By way of art, arcane, refined
And by your favour grant
Thy beauteous mien unto my pen
That we may as one find grace
And Peace

Sunny Lemon Cookies

by Rebecca Buchanan

Lemon cookies are a favorite in my household, especially when served with blueberry frosting. They also make an appropriate offering for Apollo, either plain or when marked with one of His symbols.

Ingredients
1/2 cup butter, melted
3/4 cup sugar
2 tablespoons brown sugar
1 egg
2 tablespoons lemon juice
1 tablespoon lemon bakery emulsion
1 tablespoon honey
2 cups flour
2 teaspoons dried lemon peel (optional)
pinch of salt
1 teaspoon baking soda

Combine the butter, sugar, brown sugar, egg, and lemon juice in a bowl, and mix well. Add the bakery emulsion and honey, mixing well. Add the flour, optional dried lemon peel, and pinch of salt. The mixture should be firm, but not dry, and still malleable. Add the baking soda and more lemon juice, to taste, as needed. Mix again.

Spoon the mixture onto a baking tray using an ice cream scoop, or spoon. Flatten the balls of dough with a spatula.

Inscribe symbols associated with Apollo into the dough, using a knife or toothpick or stamp. A few examples include: sun, sunflower, dolphin, lyre, flute, raven, wolf. Alternatively, after the cookies are baked, use a cut-out pattern to place powdered sugar shapes on the cookies, or make shapes out of frosting.

Bake for eight to ten minutes at 350 degrees. Serve warm.

Thargelia for Solitaries

by Samantha Lykeia Sanders

As the seasons cycle around we note the absence and return of the daughter of Demeter as life declines and returns. We also acknowledge an overlapping cycle as the sun's light increases, reaches it's height, and then falls again into darkness. Anyone who grows plants knows how important light is; it is this light that creates a growing season that brings plants into their fruitfulness and the waning light in autumn that brings late vegetables into their own ripeness. In some areas of the world certain foods cannot be grown because of the length of the growing season, and yet other foods can reach mammoth proportions because of the rulership of light in the sky (these being mostly vegetables).

With the first blush of summer, when Thargelia occurs, we are aware of two things: the changing of the seasons with the beginning of the Sun's ascent, and the fruitfulness of many plants already (depending on where you live, of course). The longer hours of sunlight stimulate the fertility of the plants. Yet for something to be productive it must be purified, as in the early spring/late winter festival of Lupercalia, which was primarily a purification ritual, but which also celebrated life and fertility.

In human experience we know that to begin something new, it is often necessary to purge the old which would be detrimental to our own continued growth. So likewise for Thargelia we celebrate both purification and crops. We can recall the Pythian Apollon destroying the plague-bringing serpent Python, and yet the waters that rose from its blood nourished the land; we can also acknowledge the valuable assistance of Apollon in the growth of food-stuff to fill our bellies.

Celebrating the Thargelia

Typically the Thargelia is held over two days during the lunar month Thargelion. The first day of Thargelia starts with the holy day of Artemis, the sixth of the month. This is the day for the purification of the community, and so it is good to remember not only Apollon who strikes down the ills, but also Artemis as a goddess purification. On this first day a man and woman would traditionally be chosen to act as *pharmakos*, and after being walked around the community they would be removed and abandoned, acting as scapegoats that had absorbed all the ills of the community.

Now this may cause some modern practitioners to balk, but there are ways to incorporate the *pharmakos* into the ritual in a satisfactory manner; and that would be through building one. There are many ways you can go about this. You can make a cloth doll, carve a human figure, buy clay, or even make a sort of "modeling clay" available from household ingredients for which there are many recipes available online. Here is one such recipe that makes a crude but quick doll that is bio-degradable and therefore safe if you wish to abandon it, burn it, or bury it.

1/2 cup potato starch, or corn starch
1 cup salt
1 cup boiling water

Boil the mixture until it is similar to a soft-ball; then knead on waxed paper. Wrap the clay in a wet cloth, and place in air-tight container to keep it moist. Once it is finished allow it air dry for at least twenty-four hours.

If you feel inclined you may add personal ingredients to the *pharmakos* as it will serve mostly for your singular purification (unless you are living in a large community or there are going to be many people participating). I would also recommend that you not feel pressured to take the doll around your entire community. It would serve quite well to take it around the property where you live, or, if you are feeling ambitious, the block you live on.

It is sometimes necessary to strike the *pharmakos* for the betterment of your being, as is reflected by the Python. Serpents are sacred to Apollon, and this destroying god who could ravish with plagues also destroyed the Python, the plague of men and livestock. At the outset it may seem entirely negative in purpose and design, but it is a necessary part of the ritual.

After finishing your trek you may dispose of the doll in whatever way you decide is best, though burning seems to be the preferred method.

In recognition of Artemis on her day, and correlating nicely to the purification ritual of the *pharmakos*, you may want to incorporate some the ritual elements of her festival as Artemis Orthia in Sparta. On this day cheese would be laid upon the altar of Artemis guarded by men bearing whips. In Spartan fashion, boys transitioning and preparing for adulthood lived apart from their families and these boys would go to steal the cheese from the altar. Invariably they were caught and whipped.

What may seem like a brutal practice to modern sensibilities actually served a purpose. These boys were leaving childhood for an adulthood as a warrior. They were slowly being purged of the softness of youth. It is quite possible that this whipping served as a form of purification.

Scourging is not unknown historically for purification of oneself, and can be used quite effectively for these purposes if you have a mind to try it. I recommend it, for, in the end, despite the stinging skin, there is a wondrous feeling of being able to breathe more easily, of a new life in the body. If you have another person handy who is willing and whom you trust, you can have them flog you across the back; or, if no one is available, self-flogging is rather simple and you will be able to reach most places with your scourge.

Participants in the Thargelia may also follow a flogging with a purification bath (or skip the flogging and bathe instead) in remembrance of the goddess bathing and renewing herself.

The second day of Thargelia is the holy day of Apollon, and is marked by the offering of first fruits to the god. As remarked earlier, the fruitfulness of these plants wouldn't be possible without the hours of nurturing light shining down on them. And in southern climates it is the mid- and late-spring sun which is most beneficial, whereas in contrast the light and heat of midsummer tends to kill everything more often than not.

I recommend getting self-rising flour if you can't get barley flour and follow pretty close to basic bread instructions. Here is my adapted *thargelos*. For this recipe I would highly recommend dividing the dough into either four loaves for manageable full sized loaves of bread, or ten palm-sized loaves which are easy to share among guests, to offer in ritual, and store. You can of course add additional grains, fruits, and nuts to personalize it.

Boil approximately 1 1/2 cups of barley until soft;

Mix two packages of active rise yeast with 4 3/4 cup self rising bread flour;

Mix with two cups of water;

Dimple and top with olive oil, and let rise;

Knead in honey, raisins, cinnamon and more flour until dough is elastic;

Dimple and top with olive oil, and allow to rise again;

Divide into separate loaves;

Shape loaves;

In a bowl, mix one egg with a dash of milk;

Brush egg mixture onto the top of the loaves;

Dust with cinnamon (optional);

Bake in the oven at 350 degrees until brown.

Conclusion

In celebrating the Thargelia recall these functions of Apollon that represent why you are purifying, and why you are offering him grain through the *thargelos*. Celebrate the warmth of community spirit as you feast, for as anyone from a large Mediterranean family can tell you nearly everything revolves around the family eating together. The ills have been driven out and now you celebrate, feast, and make-merry in presence of this god who purifies, renews, and ripens plant life.

And if you want to feed left-over crumbs to the birds it certainly wouldn't be out of the ordinary.

Three Incense Recipes

by Tina Georgitsis

Apollo Oracle Incense
1 part Dried Bay Laurel
1 part Aniseed
1 part Frankincense
1 part Myrrh

Instructions: crush herbs and resins in a mortar and pestle and sprinkle over hot charcoal or throw into a fire pit. Scry using smoke or flames.

Apollo Devotional Incense
I part Raw Honey
1 part Barley
1 part Dried Bay Laurel

Instructions: crush bay in a mortar and pestle with barley. When reduced to a granulated powder, add raw honey and place flattened mixture on a plate or piece of baking paper to dry. Sprinkle a pinch over hot charcoal.

Apollo Victor Incense
1 Part Dried Hyacinth Flowers
1 Part Dried Apple Flowers
1 Part Bay Laurel
1 Part Orange Oil or Neroli Oil

Instructions: crush bay in a mortar and pestle with apple and hyacinth flowers. When reduced to a rough mixture, add orange or neroli oil and place flattened mixture on a plate or piece of baking paper to dry. Sprinkle a pinch over hot charcoal.

Apollo Altar by Devon Power

Appendix A: Public Domain Hymns

Homeric Hymn 3 to Pythian Apollo (trans. Evelyn-White) (Greek epic circa 7th to 4th B.C.):

O Lord [Apollon], Lykia (Lycia) is yours and lovely Maionian and Miletos, charming city by the sea, but over wave-girt Delos you greatly reign your own self. Leto's all-glorious son goes to rocky Pytho, playing upon his hollow lure, clad in divine, perfumed garments; and at the touch of the golden key his lyre sings sweet. Thence, swift as thought, he speeds from earth to Olympos, to the house of Zeus, to join the gathering of the other gods: then straightway the undying gods think only of the lyre and song, and all the Mousai together, voice sweetly answering voice, hymn the unending gifts the gods enjoy and the sufferings of men . . .

Meanwhile the rich-tressed Kharites (Charites, Graces) and cheerful Horai (Seasons) dance with Harmonia and Hebe and Aphrodite, daughter of Zeus, holding each other by the wrist. And among them sings one . . .

Artemis who delights in arrows, sister of Apollon. Among them sport Ares and the keen-eyed Argeiphontes [Hermes], while Apollon plays his lure stepping high and featly and radiance shines around him, the gleaming of his feet and close-woven vest. And they, even gold-tressed Leto and wise Zeus, rejoice in their great hearts as they watch their dear son playing among the undying gods.

***

Homeric Hymn 21 to Apollo:

Phoibos [Apollon], of you even the swan sings with clear voice to the beating of his wings, as he alights upon the bank by the eddying river Peneios; and of you the sweet-tongued minstrel, holding his high-pitched lyre, always sings both first and last. And so hail to you lord! I seek your favour with my song.

***

Orphic Hymn 34 to Apollo (trans. Taylor) (Greek hymns C3rd B.C. to 2nd A.D.):

To Apollon. Blest Paian (Paean), come, propitious to my prayer, illustrious power, whom Memphian tribes revere, Tityoktonos (Slayer of Tityos), and the god of Health, Lykoreus, Phoibos, fruitful source of wealth: Pytheion, golden-lyred, the field from thee receives its constant rich fertility. Titan, Gryneion, Smyntheus, thee I sing, Pythoktonos (Python-Slayer), hallowed, Delphion king: rural, light-bearing Daimon, and Mousagetos (Leader of the Mousai, or Muses), noble and lovely, armed with arrows dread: far-darting, Bakkhion, twofold and divine, power far diffused, and course oblique is thine.

O Delian king, whose light-producing eye views all within, and all beneath the sky; whose locks are gold, whose oracles are sure, who omens good revealest, and precepts pure; hear me entreating for he human kind, hear, and be present with benignant mind; for thou surveyest this boundless aither all, and every part of this terrestrial ball abundant, blessed; and thy piercing sight extends beneath the gloomy, silent night; Beyond the darkness, starry-eyed, profound, the table roots, deep-fixed by thee, are found.

The world's wide bounds, all-flourishing, are thine, thyself of all the source and end divine. 'Tis thine all nature's music to inspire with various-sounding, harmonious lyre: now the last string thou tunest to sweet accord, divinely warbling, now the highest chord; the immortal golden lyre, now touched by thee, responsive yields a Dorian melody.

All nature's tribes to thee their difference owe, and changing seasons from thy music flow: hence, mixed by thee in equal parts, advance summer and winter in alternate dance; this claims the highest, that the lowest string, the Dorian measure tunes the lovely spring: hence by mankind Pan royal, two-horned named, shrill winds emitting through the syrinx famed; since to thy care the figured seal's consigned, which stamps the world with forms of every kind.

Hear me, blest power, and in these rites rejoice, and save thy mystics with a suppliant voice.

***

Philostratus the Elder, Imagines 2. 19 (trans. Fairbanks) (Greek rhetorician C3rd A.D.) :

As for the aspect of the god [Apollon], he is represented as unshorn, my boy, and with his hair fastened up so that he may box with girt-up head; rays of light rise from about his brow and his cheek emits a smile mingled with wrath; keen is the glance of his eyes as it follows his uplifted hands.

***

Philostratus the Younger, Imagines 14 (trans. Fairbanks) (Greek rhetorician C3rd A.D.) :

[From a description of an ancient Greek painting:] Here is the god [Apollon], painted as usual with unshorn locks; he lifts a radiant forehead above eyes that shine like rays of light.

Appendix B: Recommended Reading

Apollo by Fritz Graf
Apollo: God of the Sun, Healing, Music, and Poetry by Teri Temple
Apollo the Brilliant One by George O'Connor
Gods in Everyman by Jean Shinoda Bolen
The Gods of the Greeks by Karl Kerenyi
The Golden God by Doris Gates
The Mask of Apollo by Mary Renault
Treasury of Greek Mythology by Donna Jo Napoli and Christina Balit
The Trials of Apollo by Rick Riordan

Appendix C: Our Contributors

Gary Beck has spent most of his adult life as a theater director, and as an art dealer when he couldn't make a living in theater. He has published eleven chapbooks. His poetry collections include: *Days of Destruction* (*Skive Press*), *Expectations* (*Rogue Scholars Press*). *Dawn in Cities, Assault on Nature, Songs of a Clerk, Civilized Ways, Displays* (*Winter Goose Publishing*). *Fault Lines, Perceptions, Tremors, Perturbations, Rude Awakenings* and *The Remission of Order* will be published by *Winter Goose Publishing. Conditioned Response* (*Nazar Look*). *Resonance* (*Dreaming Big Publications*). His novels include: *Extreme Change* (*Cogwheel Press*) and *Flawed Connections* (*Black Rose Writing*). *Call to Valor* will be published by *Gnome on Pigs Productions* and *Acts of Defiance* will be published by *Dreaming Big Publications*. His short story collection is *A Glimpse of Youth* (*Sweatshoppe Publications*). *Now I Accuse* and other stories will be published by *Winter Goose Publishing*. His original plays and translations of Moliere, Aristophanes, and Sophocles have been produced Off Broadway. His poetry, fiction and essays have appeared in hundreds of literary magazines. He currently lives in New York City.

Kayleigh Ayn Bohémier is a Hellenic Polytheist who lives in New England. Her poetry has appeared in *Goblin Fruit, Eternal Haunted Summer,* and *Astropoetica.*

John J. Brugaletta has published three book-length collections of his poetry, the latest of which is *With My Head Rising out of the Water* (Negative Capability Press, 2014).

Rebecca Buchanan is the editor of the Pagan literary ezine, *Eternal Haunted Summer.* She is also the editor-in-chief of *Bibliotheca Alexandrina.* She has been published in a wide variety of venues, including *Bards and Sages Quarterly, Enheduanna, Nebula Rift, New Realm,* and *The Future Fire,* among others.

Ellen Denton is a freelance writer living in the Rocky Mountains with her husband and two demonic cats that wreak havoc and hell (the cats, not the husband). Her fiction and non-fiction short stories have been published in over a hundred magazines and anthologies. She has also had an exciting life working as a circus acrobat, a CIA spy, a service provider in the Red Light District, a navy seal, a ballerina on the starship Enterprise, and was the first person to climb Mount Everest. (Editorial note: The publication credits are true, but some of the other stuff above may be fictional.)

Amanda Artemisia Forrester, formerly Amanda Sioux Blake, is currently in transition from the

Indiana/Michigan area to the Missouri homestead of her dreams. She is the author of *Ink In My Veins: A Collection of Contemporary Pagan Poetry* and *Songs of Praise: Hymns to the Gods of Greece*. She is working on the forthcoming *Journey to Olympos: A Modern Spiritual Odyssey*. A self-labeled history geek, she has taught classes on Greek Mythology, contacting your spirit guides, and has written and taught the coursework for *Olympos in Egypt*, an introduction to the unique hybrid culture and spiritually that grew up in Alexandria, Egypt in the Hellenistic Age. In a few years when the homestead is up and running, she may make it her goal to begin teaching again and holding rituals on her 5 acre property, Artemis Acres, and reestablish the Temple of Athena the Savior in Missouri. Her blog can be found at templeofathena.wordpress.com, and she runs a Cafepress store, OtherWorld Creations, at cafepress.com/other_world.

All her life, **Tina Georgitsis** has maintained a deep love and appreciation for the occult, whilst also being deeply respectful to the Ancient Greek and Ancient Egyptian spiritual/magickal paths which she is devoted to. She is an Arch Priestess Hierophant within the FOI (Lyceum of Heka), Hereditary Folk/Hermetic Witch, Initiated Wiccan Priestess and runs the Sanctuary of Hekate's Crossroads (a temple devoted to Hekate) and is the owner of Hekate's Crossroads (a popular Facebook group devoted to Hekate). Qualified as a Reiki,

Seichim and Sekhem Master and Tarot Councillor with the ATA, Tina has also studied various modalities within natural/alternative medicine and operates a spiritually based business (Setjataset) which includes readings, healings, magickal items and workshops in various metaphysical and occult subjects. Tina has been published in several various publications over the years ranging from anthologies, magazines and blogs. A regular article writer focusing on Kemetic, Hellenic and general occult works, she also edited her first book, *Daughter of the Sun: A Devotional Anthology in Honor of Sekhmet* in 2015.

Joe Giordano's stories have appeared in more than eighty magazines including *Bartleby Snopes*, *The Monarch Review, decomP,* and *Shenandoah.* His novel, *Birds of Passage, An Italian Immigrant Coming of Age Story*, was published by *Harvard Square Editions* October 2015. Read the first chapter and sign up for his blog at http://joe-giordano.com/

Neile Graham grew up in scraps of forest on the west coast of Canada. She writes poems and novels, holds an MFA in writing, and attended Clarion West Writers Workshop, where she currently serves as its workshop director. Her poetry collections include *Spells for Clear Vision* and *Blood Memory*, and a spoken word cd.

Audrey Greathouse is the author of many science-fiction and fantasy stories, including her debut novel, *The Neverland Wars*. A lost child in a perpetual and footloose quest for her own post-adolescent Neverland, Audrey has grand hopes for the future which include publishing more books and owning a crockpot.

A.J. Huffman has published twelve full-length poetry collections, thirteen solo poetry chapbooks, and one joint poetry chapbook through a variety of small presses. Among her most recent releases are *Degeneration* (*Pink Girl Ink*), *A Bizarre Burning of Bees* (*Transcendent Zero Press*), and *Familiar Illusions* (*Flutter Press*), which are now available from their respective publishers. She is a five-time Pushcart Prize nominee, a two-time Best of Net nominee, and has published over 2500 poems in various national and international journals, including *Labletter, The James Dickey Review, The Bookends Review, Bone Orchard, Corvus Review, EgoPHobia,* and *Kritya*. She is also the founding editor of *Kind of a Hurricane Press*, which can be found at www.kindofahurricanepress.com.

Callum Hurley is a Biological researcher living in beautiful Yorkshire, England. Whilst a Scientist by profession he has always possessed a deep, abiding love of both poetry and mythology from a young age. Particularly found of Hermetic thought and aesthetic, he has contributed to numerous

Bibliotheca Alexandria projects over the years, and hopes to continue to do so for the years to come.

Jason Ross Inczauskis completed his Masters degree in Plant Biology and is currently residing in Southern Illinois. He currently lives in a small house with his love, Tabitha, and more books and dolls than you can shake a stick at. He has worshipped Athena since the year 2000, and gradually came to worship the other Hellenic deities as well, officially converting to Hellenismos in 2010. When asked about his spiritual path, he may refer to himself as a Hellene, a Hellenic Polytheist, an Orphic, or Greek Pre-Orthodox, depending on who's asking and his mood at the time, though he always follows it with the caveat: 'but not a very good one'. He is the editor for *Shield of Wisdom: A Devotional Anthology in Honor of Athena*. His devotional writing has also appeared in *He Epistole*, as well as several books, including *From Cave to Sky: A Devotional Anthology in Honor of Zeus, Queen of Olympos: A Devotional Anthology for Hera and Iuno, Harnessing Fire: A Devotional Anthology in Honor of Hephaestus, Guardian of the Road: A Devotional Anthology in Honor of Hermes, Out of Arcadia: A Devotional Anthology in Honor of Pan, Unto Herself: A Devotional Anthology for Independent Goddesses, The Scribing Ibis: An Anthology of Pagan Fiction in Honor of Thoth*, and *The Shining Cities: An Anthology of Pagan Science Fiction*.

Steven Klepetar's work has appeared widely and has received several nominations for Best of the Net and the Pushcart Prize. Recent collections include *My Son Writes a Report on the Warsaw Ghetto* and *The Li Bo Poems*, both from *Flutter Press*, and *Family Reunion*, forthcoming from *Big Table Publishing*.

An artist, author, ritualist, presenter, and spiritual seeker, **Shauna Aura Knight** travels nationally offering intensive education in the transformative arts of ritual, community leadership, and personal growth. She is the author of *The Leader Within*, *Ritual Facilitation*, and *Dreamwork for the Initiate's Path*, and co-editor of the *Pagan Leadership Anthology*. Her writing is included in several blogs and Pagan magazines, and her work appears in numerous anthologies including *Pagan Consent Culture*, *Bringing Race to the Table*, *Stepping in to Ourselves*, and more.

She's also the author of urban fantasy and paranormal romance novels including *The Truth Upon Her Lips*, *A Fading Amaranth*, *A Winter Knight's Vigil*, *Werewolves in the Kitchen*, *Werewolves with Chocolate*, and more. Shauna's mythic artwork and designs are used for magazine covers, book covers, and illustrations, as well as decorating many walls, shrines, and other spaces. Shauna is passionate about creating rituals, experiences, spaces, stories, and artwork to awaken mythic imagination. Check out her site at http://www.shaunaauraknight.com

Maggie Koger is a Media Specialist with a writing habit. She lives and works in Boise and celebrates Le Bois — the trees the city is named for. She has published poetry in *Poet Lore, Avocet, Mused, WestWard Quarterly, Montucky*, and *Eternal Haunted Summer*.

Terence Kuch's fiction and poetry has appeared in numerous university-affiliated and other periodicals including *Best Fiction, Blinking Cursor (UK), Commonweal, Copperfield Review, Diagram, Foundling Review, Gravel, Hobble Creek Review, New York magazine, North American Review, Penguin Review, Salt River Review, Sheepshead Review, Slant, Stray Branch, The Moth (Eire)*, and *Timber Creek Review*.

Jennifer Lawrence has followed the gods of Greece, Ireland, and the Northlands for decades now; she is a member of Hellenion, The Troth, Ár nDraíocht Féin, and Ord Brigideach. Her interests include history, gardening, herbalism, mythology and fairy tales, hiking, camping, and the martial arts. Her work has appeared in numerous publications, including *Aphelion, Jabberwocky, Cabinet Des Fees, Goblin Fruit, Idunna, Oak Leaves,* and many devotional anthologies. She lives with five cats, an overgrown garden full of nature spirits, and a houseful of gargoyles somewhere outside of Chicago.

Nicole Lungeanu is a dedicated vet nurse living with her beautiful wife in Braunschweig, Germany. She's a land-locked mermaid and dancer who enjoys a good cup of coffee or tea, chocolate, writing smutty stuff, reading in bed, and life in general. Her drawings have been published in various magazines in Germany and Great Britain, such as *Animania* and *Exposé*. She also loves to write romance. Her first novel, *Sonnenstaub,* tells the story of a young woman and her relationship with the Greek Gods, especially Apollon. The book is on its way to getting published and the sequel is already in progress. Her way of living has changed profoundly since Hermes found His way into her life. You can find more of her artwork on: nerhegeb1981.deviantart.com and her writing on nicoleschreibtauf.wordpress.com (in German).

Sabina Lungeanu was born in Romania and is currently living in Germany. She has a degree in Biology and speaks four languages. Ancient history has been a constant source of inspiration to her. The Greek pantheon holds a special place in her heart, and Apollon most of all. During a trip to Greece, she fulfilled a longtime dream to visit Delphi, which remains to this day her favourite place to be. Several poems featured in this anthology have been written on that sacred ground, under the shadow of the Parnassian peaks. Though her first love was poetry, Sabina has also discovered the joys of writing prose. Her first novel draws heavily upon the myths and legends of her native land, shedding light on the little known, but fascinating culture of the Dacians.

Hillary Lyon is founder of and editor for *Subsynchronous Press*, publisher of the poetry journals *The Laughing Dog*, and *Veil: Journal of Darker Musings*. Author of over twenty chapbooks, her poems have appeared in print, online, and in anthologies. She lives in the healing sunshine of Southern Arizona.

Mari is a Hellenic polytheist residing in south Louisiana. She has been writing poetry for nearly two decades and has published two collections of devotional poems and prayers for the gods of Hellenic polytheism. *Glories* and *Laureate* are available through lulu.com as paperbacks and ebooks.

T.J. O'Hare writes short stories, novels, song lyrics, poetry, plays and film scripts. His novel *Amnesiak: Blood Divinity* published by *Spero Publications* is at https://www.smashwords.com/books/view/260414. He co-writes with many musical collaborators. His plays have been staged in Northern Ireland and Belgium. He is married to

Jean, and has two grown-up sons. He lives in the north of Ireland.

Dr. John "Apollonius" Opsopaus has practiced magic, divination, and Neopaganism since the 1960s. He has more than thirty publications in various magical and Neopagan magazines; he designed the Pythagorean Tarot and wrote the comprehensive *Guide to the Pythagorean Tarot* (Llewellyn, 2001). Opsopaus frequently presents workshops on Hellenic magic and Neopaganism, Pythagorean theurgy, divination, and related topics. In 1995, Dr. Opsopaus founded the Omphalos, a networking organization for Graeco-Roman Neopagans, and his Biblioteca Arcana website has won numerous awards. He is a Third Circle member of the Church of All Worlds and past coordinator of the Scholars Guild for CAW; he was also Arkhon of the Hellenic Kin of ADF (A Druid Fellowship). Opsopaus is a member of the Grey Council and is past Dean of the Departments of Mathemagicks and Ceremonial Magick of the Grey School of Wizardry. His writings can be found at www.omphalos.org/BA.

Jessica Orlando opted not to provide a biography.

Hélio Pires is a Portuguese Roman polytheist and Mercury devotee who has been a worshipper of Freyr for over a decade. He never identified the son of Njord with any Mediterranean deity, creating a

Romanized cult instead, but the experience made evident several commonalities between Apollo and Freyr. He's a Medieval historian, avid biker, an occasional boomerang thrower, very keen on moving through sunny outdoors with a backpack, sings Monty Python songs when he's had a bit too much to drink, and enjoys piling rocks by the side of the road. Also, don't ask him about the long-term unfolding and interconnectedness of historical events, because he can go on about it for hours!

Devon Power opted not to provide a biography.

Michael Routery is a Celtic polytheist, druid, and practitioner of *filidecht,* as well as a devotee of a number of Hellenic deities. He's the author of *From the Prow of Myth*, a book of devotional poetry. Some of his poems and essays can be found in various *Bibliotheca Alexandrina* anthologies, including *Seasons of Grace; By Blood, Bone and Blade; Written in Wine; Out of Arcadia;* and *The Scribing Ibis*. More can be found in the *Scarlet Imprint* volumes *Mandragora* and *Datura*. Michael blogs at finnchuillsmast.wordpress.com.

K.S. Roy (also known as Khryseis Astra) is an artist, astrologer and writer living in Western Pennsylvania. She is particularly devoted to Hekate, Hermes, Persephone, Apollon and the Muses. She has been Graphic Designer for *He Epistole*, a Hellenic Polytheist newsletter issued by Neokoroi, the Editor for *Guardian of the Road: A Devotional Anthology in Honor of Hermes* and creates devotional art for the Theoi.

Samantha Lykeia Sanders opted not to provide a biography.

Host of the Gelato Poetry Series, author of the poetry collection *Words of Power Dances of Freedom*, and an editor of the *San Diego Poetry Annual*, **Jon Wesick** has published over three hundred poems in journals such as the *Atlanta Review, Pearl,* and *Slipstream.* He has also published nearly a hundred short stories. One was nominated for a Pushcart Prize. One of his poems won second place in the 2007 African American Writers and Artists contest. Another had a link on the *Car Talk* website.

Gareth Writer-Davies was Commended in the Prole Laureate Competition in 2015, Specially Commended in the Welsh Poetry Competition and Highly Commended in the Sherborne Open Poetry Competition. Shortlisted for the Bridport Prize and the Erbacce Prize in 2014. His pamphlet *Bodies*, was published in 2015 through *Indigo Dreams*. His next pamphlet, *Cry Baby*, will be released in 2017.

Appendix D: About Bibliotheca Alexandrina

Ptolemy Soter, the first Makedonian ruler of Egypt, established the library at Alexandria to collect all of the world's learning in a single place. His scholars compiled definitive editions of the Classics, translated important foreign texts into Greek, and made monumental strides in science, mathematics, philosophy and literature. By some accounts over a million scrolls were housed in the famed library, and though it has long since perished due to the ravages of war, fire, and human ignorance, the image of this great institution has remained as a powerful inspiration down through the centuries.

To help promote the revival of traditional polytheistic religions we have launched a series of books dedicated to the ancient gods of Greece and Egypt. The library is a collaborative effort drawing on the combined resources of the different elements within the modern Hellenic and Kemetic communities, in the hope that we can come together to praise our gods and share our diverse understandings, experiences and approaches to the divine.

A list of our current and forthcoming titles can be found on the following page. For more information on the Bibliotheca, our submission requirements for upcoming devotionals, or to learn about our organization, please visit us at neosalexandria.org.

Sincerely,

The Editorial Board
of the Library of Neos Alexandria

Current Titles
Written in Wine: A Devotional Anthology for
      Dionysos
Dancing God: Poetry of Myths and Magicks
Goat Foot God
Longing for Wisdom: The Message of the Maxims
The Phillupic Hymns
Unbound: A Devotional Anthology for Artemis
Waters of Life: A Devotional Anthology for Isis and
      Serapis
Bearing Torches: A Devotional Anthology for
      Hekate
Queen of the Great Below: An Anthology in Honor
      of Ereshkigal
From Cave to Sky: A Devotional Anthology in
      Honor of Zeus
Out of Arcadia: A Devotional Anthology for Pan
Anointed: A Devotional Anthology for the Deities
      of the Near and Middle East
The Scribing Ibis: An Anthology of Pagan Fiction in
      Honor of Thoth

Queen of the Sacred Way: A Devotional Anthology
in Honor of Persephone
Unto Herself: A Devotional Anthology for
Independent Goddesses
The Shining Cities: An Anthology of Pagan Science
Fiction
Guardian of the Road: A Devotional Anthology in
Honor of Hermes
Harnessing Fire: A Devotional Anthology in Honor
of Hephaestus
Beyond the Pillars: An Anthology of Pagan Fantasy
Queen of Olympos: A Devotional Anthology for
Hera and Iuno
A Mantle of Stars: A Devotional Anthology in
Honor of the Queen of Heaven
Crossing the River: An Anthology in Honor of
Sacred Journeys
Ferryman of Souls: A Devotional for Charon
By Blood, Bone, and Blade: A Tribute to the
Morrigan
Potnia: An Anthology in Honor of Demeter
The Queen of the Sky Who Rules Over All the
Gods: A Devotional Anthology in Honor of
Bast
From the Roaring Deep: A Devotional for Poseidon
and the Spirits of the Sea
Daughter of the Sun: A Devotional Anthology in
Honor of Sekhmet
Seasons of Grace: A Devotional in Honor of the
Muses, the Charites, and the Horae
Lunessence: A Devotional for Selene

Les Cabinets des Polythéistes: An Anthology of
    Pagan Fairy Tales, Folktales, and Nursery
    Rhymes
With Lyre and Bow: A Devotional in Honor of
    Apollo

Forthcoming Titles
Garland of the Goddess: Tales and Poems of the
    Feminine Divine
Dauntless: A Devotional in Honor of Ares and Mars
The Dark Ones: Tales and Poems of the Shadow
    Gods
First and Last: A Devotional for Hestia
Blood and Roses: A Devotional in Honor of
    Aphrodite
At the Gates of Dawn and Dusk: A Devotional for
    Eos and Aurora
The Far-Shining One: A Devotional in Honor of
    Helios and the Spirits of the Sun
Shield of Wisdom: A Devotional Anthology in
    Honor of Athena
Megaloi Theoi: A Devotional Anthology for the
    Dioskouroi and Their Families
Sirius Rising: A Devotional Anthology for
    Cynocephalic Deities

CPSIA information can be obtained
at www.ICGtesting.com
Printed in the USA
LVHW031649201122
733652LV00008B/609

9 781535 388207